TRAGEDY
in the
SHENANDOAH VALLEY

To Stewart -
Merry Christmas from Jerdy -
Best Wishes -
[signature]
11/12/00

TRAGEDY
in the
SHENANDOAH VALLEY

The Story of the
Summers-Koontz Execution

ROBERT H. MOORE II

Charleston · London

History
PRESS

Published by The History Press
Charleston, SC 29403
www.historypress.net

Cover Image: Summers-Koontz Monument, just north of New Market along Route 11 (Valley Turnpike) at Rude's Hill in Shenandoah County, Virginia.

First published 2006

Manufactured in the United Kingdom

ISBN 1.59629.165.6

Moore, Robert H.
  Tragedy in the Shenandoah Valley : the story of the Summers-Koontz execution / Robert H. Moore, II.
     p. cm.
  Includes bibliographical references and index.
  ISBN 1-59629-165-6 (alk. paper)
  1. Summers, George W., d. 1865. 2. Koontz, Isaac Newton, d. 1865. 3. Confederate States of America. Army. Virginia Cavalry Regiment, 7th. Company D--Demobilization. 4. Executions and executioners--Virginia--Page County--History--19th century. 5. Page County (Va.)--History, Military--19th century. 6. Virginia--History--Civil War, 1861-1865. 7. United States--History--Civil War, 1861-1865. I. Title.
  E581.67th .M66 2006
  973.7'455--dc22

                         2006021092

To Sergeant Isaac Newton Koontz's fiancée, Emma Jane Shuler Strole
(1846–1912)
Who was also my great-great-great-grandmother

Also to each generation of her children and grandchildren including:
Her daughter—Clara Virginia Strole Roudabush (1872–1954)
Her granddaughter—Charlotte Virginia Roudabush Moore (1897–1981)
Her great-grandson—Robert Fenton Moore (born 1915)
And her great-great-grandson and my father, Robert Hume Moore (born 1943)
And to all succeeding generations that follow,
With the hope that they will long remember this story.

Contents

Acknowledgements

After well over a decade of compiling information about the Summers-Koontz incident, I have a number of people and organizations to thank. Many of these have been very generous in allowing the use of photographs, including John and Sandie Hammel, the Kansas State Historical Society, Philip D. Lusk, Janet Koontz Robinson, Joann Schaub, Tom Stumph, Janice Taylor, Ann Vaughn and Stephen E. Williams. For access to various manuscripts, or related documents and stories, I also thank Barbara Austen of the Connecticut Historical Society, Jeb Caudill of the *Page News & Courier*, John L. Heatwole, Colonel Bill and Frances Menefee, Violet Mitchell, the Library of Virginia, the National Archives and the United States Army Military History Institute. Barbara Petite was also instrumental in working with me to locate and copy the pension files of the Union officers involved in this incident. Furthermore, thanks go to the late Alice Wolfersberger Foltz who was so generous in allowing free and regular access to the Summers-Strole Cemetery at Grove Hill. Last but not least, to the members of the Summers-Koontz Camp No. 490, with whom I have spent a great deal of time in the past six years learning more and perpetuating the legacy of Captain Summers and Sergeant Koontz.

Certainly, my wife and children have been very patient with me while involved in this project and played a critical role in my achieving success in completing this work. As always, they have my undying love, but for the completion of this work and all other works, as ever, I owe them my utmost thanks.

I also thank God for seeing me through this work.

Lastly, if I have in any way accidentally omitted someone else for whom I owed a debt of gratitude for assistance in this work in one way or another, I extend my apologies and hope that the very completion of this work will be acceptable thanks to those who might remain nameless.

A Note to the Reader

Several years back, during my youth, I read the brief account of the Summers-Koontz incident in Harry M. Strickler's *Short History of Page County*, but not until sometime later and after several years of research did I realize that a primary character in the story—Emma Jane Shuler—was also my great-great-great-grandmother. This of course left me mystified as to why I had never heard about the story through any family members. Of the two generations of daughters that had descended from Emma, considering that she did not die until 1912, certainly the story of the Summers-Koontz incident would have been passed along on many occasions, as telling stories of the past in that day and age, especially before the advent of the television, was commonplace among many families. Nevertheless, at some point in time, those stories, at least in my family line, dissipated as the generations rolled on. Certainly, this was a major factor in my ever-pressing desire to commit many more years toward learning more about the incident.

While the personal mystery of why I never heard about the story will probably remain just that, after years of researching the incident and filling in where lack of oral accounts left me hungry for more information, with each new piece of evidence revealed, I came to appreciate the many ironies that dotted the story. The largest irony brings to mind Robert Frost's poem, "The Road Not Taken" (1915) along with a little bit of George Bailey in *It's a Wonderful Life* (1946). Had any number of events gone differently leading up to the execution of June 27, 1865, things might have gone quite differently, and perhaps Isaac Newton Koontz may have survived; in which case, it leaves one to wonder if descendants of Emma Jane Shuler—myself included—would have been here today.

Nevertheless, when I first wrote about the Summers-Koontz incident well over a decade ago, I wrote a much smaller story based on a small number of accounts and minor details outlining events leading up to the execution of Captain George W. Summers and Sergeant Isaac Newton Koontz on June 27, 1865. From the moment that I had completed the first account, I knew that there was more of a story that could be told, a much larger story, but I simply didn't have any resources on hand to back up that desire. Over time, and after some accidental findings in the course of research on other topics pertaining to the history of Page County, Virginia, I came to realize that this tragic execution has a much more complex and interesting story. This is not simply a story of a postwar tragedy, but more importantly how what amounted to a secondary war between civilians—outspoken Unionists and "fire-eating secessionists"—in addition to the ongoing larger war on the battlefields likely proved to be a central reason behind the sad fates that befell Captain Summers and Sergeant Koontz.

Another thing I wish to point out to the reader is that, in addition to the seven chapters dedicated to the tale of Summers and Koontz, please be sure to look at the very extensive endnotes. As a matter of fact, I encourage the reader to read through the story initially without looking at the endnotes, and then read the story a second time with the endnotes. It is a bit unconventional, but I believe that reading the book in such a way actually gives the reader an opportunity to enjoy the story initially for what it is, without taking away from the story itself, and then, in the re-read, allows the reader to take a second journey into a deeper understanding of people, places and events that surround the story.

But without further adieu, in the words and spirit of Captain Andrew Jackson "Jack" Adams, it is my sincere hope, that through this book, many more will have the opportunity to reflect upon the "courage and fortitude, and the tragic deaths of Capt. Summers and Sergt. Koontz will long live in the memories of our citizens and deserve to be recited in song and story—to show what atrocities our people suffered in war, and how heroically these men met their untimely fate."

"A Voice From the Ground"

By Cornelia Jane Matthews Jordan[1]

Forget us not, us who are lying here
In slumber deep and dismal, darkness drear,
The while your busy footsteps onward pass
Above us through the tangled, waving grass
That hides us low; pause near the lonely spot,
And in your joy of life forget us not.

Forget us not who once were glad as you
'Mid the bright sunshine and the glistening dew,
Walking abroad, loving the teeming earth,
With all its glow of beauty, sounds of mirth,
Till, for your sakes, and with no slavish fear,
We met the direful fate that laid us here.
Forget us not—we do not ask to be
Like haunting ghosts marring your human glee;
But as in Memory, holy things are kept,
O'er which Affection's loyal tears are wept,
So in your hearts' deep hidden shrines and dear
We would be cherished who are sleeping here.

Forget us not, as side by side we lie,
Nor pass our lonely mounds unheeded by,
For though our palsied, mouldering hands uphold
No more our blood-stained Banner's tattered fold,
Still through the ages while to us remain
Your loving tears, we have not died in vain.

Forget us not—but as the years roll by
Bring the sweet offerings love would ne'er deny—
The buds and blossoms of the joyous May—
And on our lowly graves your tributes lay,
And say to strangers and to children dear,—
"These did their duty who are lying here."

A Community at War: Reflections of Alma and Grove Hill

In south-central Page County, just past the tenth bend in the South Fork of the Shenandoah River, one can reach the once thriving little communities of Alma and Honeyville, where two major turnpikes—the Luray to Staunton Turnpike and the Blue Ridge or New Market to Gordonsville Turnpike—once met, not far from the Columbia Bridge. Taking the same name as Noah Kite's Mill, which stood nearby, this spectacular covered bridge of two 145-five foot spans also stood not far from the homes of Isaac and Anna Keyser Koontz and Daniel and Elizabeth Mauck Koontz. Just south of this point and beyond the village of Newport is Grove Hill, near where the homes of George and Susannah Summers and Andrew Jackson Kite and his wife stood. Then, down along the Grove Hill River Road, near where the beautiful covered Red Bridge spanned the South Fork, could be found the home of "Squire" John Shuler.

All of the places and people are gone now, and to sit quietly along the banks of the South Fork of the Shenandoah River in this portion of Page County and listen to the serene sound of rippling waters cross river rocks, it is hard to imagine the tragedy that once struck this area so long ago.

At the time of the War Between the States, a good number of the eligible men who lived between Alma and Grove Hill were absent in the service of the Confederate Army, leaving several civilians, old and young, to see to matters at home. These remaining people encountered a totally different set of experiences than the soldiers in dealing with the crisis that was very much a war on the homefront. The communities in which they lived also continued to play a vital role in the county's agricultural and iron ore production.[2] Both the bounty of the harvests and the two close-by turnpikes guaranteed a place for both of these communities in Page County's role as an "avenue of armies."

Ca. 1930 view of a portion of the Blue Ridge Turnpike. Marken and Bielfeld postcard. *Courtesy of the author.*

Summers's farm landscape. *Courtesy of the author.*

The portion of Page County known as Alma District 1 reached from the village of Alma proper, east to Honeyville and south to Columbia Mills and across the river as far as Newport. Just to the south of this was Grove Hill, which covered less area in square miles but stretched to a point near where the active iron ore community of Shenandoah Iron Works began as a separate district. Naturally, as the Shenandoah Valley was the "breadbasket of the Confederacy," grain farming was king in this area, as reflected through the dominating occupations shown in both adjoining districts.

In Alma District 1, out of 120 families, there were no less than 43 farms, several of which were of significant size. Supporting this was a healthy force of laborers, millers, millwrights, coopers, colliers, shoemakers, merchants and various other persons in important roles. In addition to farming, Catherine Furnace employed a countless number of workers as well, though through their respective occupations they are not always so easily identified with the furnace. Those who can be identified with the furnace include a miner, a forgeman, a boatman and both the keeper at the furnace and the iron master himself.[3]

As in most districts in Page County, slavery had a presence in Alma; however, there were only 39 slaves in all. Out of the 120 families in this

Wheat fields near Luray, ca. 1910. *Courtesy of the Ann Vaughn Collection.*

district, 9 owned slaves. Additionally, while the total real estate value of Alma District 1 equated to $170,354, nearly half of that—$67,320—was in the hands of slave owners. Of additional note, six free blacks also resided in Alma District 1.[4]

With half the population of Alma District 1, Grove Hill had sixty-two families, consisting of twenty-three farmers, thirteen laborers and a like number of farm and community occupations.[5] As with Alma, slaves were also present in Grove Hill. With thirty-four slaves in the community, it would seem that the communities were about on par with each other. However, considering the considerably smaller number of families in Grove Hill, slaves were actually slightly more prevalent here than in Alma. Nevertheless, five out of the sixty-two families in this district owned slaves. Likewise, slave owners controlled less than a third ($41,726) of the total ($142,151) real estate value as listed in the 1860 county census. Seventeen free blacks also resided in Grove Hill.[6]

As the prospect of war continued to loom on the horizon, these communities seemed split over what to do in regard to secession. Recounting those "early days," Isaac Shuler (1849–1942), a son of Grove Hill residents John and Mary Ann Kite Shuler, remembered the two opposing parties

Shuler family wedding, November 13, 1900. Note that John Shuler is in the front row, fourth from the right. Emma Jane Shuler Strole is in the second row, second from the right. Isaac Shuler is in the back row under the porch, fourth from the left. *Courtesy of Tom Stumph.*

over the matter of secession in the county, hearing speeches "for and against it."[7] Shuler continued, "I will mention a few who took an active part in it. Peter Borst, Frank Grayson, Martin Strickler, John Dofflemoyer and others that stood for secession wanted the old State to secede and get out of the union."[8] However, he also recalled that his father, along with Luray resident John Lionberger, spoke out against secession as a hasty and unnecessary act. "Lionberger and my father were opposed to the severance of our government. To try to set up a new government or two governments would not do. If our rights had been trampled upon, let us fight under our flag the stars and stripes."

"Naturally there were speeches on both sides," wrote Shuler. John Lionberger, Dr. James L. Gillespie, Reuben M. Walton and John Shuler "spoke in opposition to it, and portrayed what the results would be if the State of Virginia seceded."[9] Isaac Shuler continued,

19

On one occasion which I will never forget, they were speaking at R.M. Walton's store at Newport. Mr. Lionberger was speaking when the crowds yelled for Squire John Shuler. He responded and in his discourse followed along the line of Lionberger, trying to impress upon the minds of his hearers the horror and bloodshed that would follow secession…

During his remarks there was a man in the audience who took an exception and made for the speaker. He dropped back in the store and grabbed a chair. R.M. Walton jumped to the counter and prevented the blow. The crowd not satisfied yelled for Shuler to again take up the speech and in his remarks said something that was displeasing to some present. They said, if we cannot get out rights in Virginia we will go to South Carolina, if we have to wade in blood up to our knees. The speaker had great respect for them and said you need not to go South Carolina where you can get all the fight in Virginia, and probably near your home.

Isaac Shuler later noted of those who said they would go to South Carolina that it was his experience that "the rooster that crows the loudest is not the best fighter. Instead of going to South Carolina when we got in to the war they remained at home and did everything they could to keep out."[10]

However, among those who remained at home, there were also a considerable number who were reluctant to relinquish their sentiment for the Union even after Abraham Lincoln's call for troops. The first test for these Unionists appears to have come when the public referendum for secession was placed before county residents in May 1861. Though the final tally of 1,099-4 seemed to declare almost absolute local support for secession, a review of the Loyalist Claims for Page County reveals several men who were reluctant to vote, but for various reasons were either coerced into voting for secession or stayed away from voting altogether. Martin Hite noted that he had been "*persuaded* to vote for the adoption of the ordinance." According to Morgan M. Price, at the time of the public referendum vote he felt that it was not safe to go to the polls and vote against secession. Price remembered that "The only man who voted against secession had to leave immediately to save himself from the mob." William H. Sours stated that "My sympathies were with the Union Cause. I did not talk much in favor of the Union. I had to be careful how I expressed my sentiment. I feared that I would be arrested if I spoke much." Samuel Varner had voted for secession because, as he claimed, he was told if he "wanted peace he must vote for secesh." Joseph Miller simply noted that he was obliged to vote for secession through "fear."[11]

Following President Abraham Lincoln's call for seventy-five thousand troops and the subsequent Ordinance of Secession passed by the Commonwealth

Captain Michael Shuler.
Courtesy of the author.

of Virginia, like a fair number of men throughout Page County, several of Alma and Grove Hill enlisted for service. Many were already enrolled in the local Ninety-seventh Virginia Militia—mostly in companies E, I, L and M. However, some local men decided to join units immediately formed for regular field service. Among the companies in which these men enlisted were Macon Jordan's Massanutten Rangers (cavalry), William D. Rippetoe's Page Grays (infantry), John K. Booton's Dixie Artillery and William T. Young's Page Volunteers (infantry).

In all, nearly 150 men from both communities had marched off to war by 1864. However, only two-thirds of that number would actually see service in regular army units, others having been activated as a part of the Ninety-seventh Virginia Militia at the opening of the war or conscripted or enrolled into the ranks of the Eighth Battalion Virginia Reserves near the war's close. Not all of the men had eagerly enlisted at the opening of the war. Some waited until later in the war and enlisted only out of the fear of embarrassment they would have to bear in the event they were drafted. At least one young man, Frederick Amos Alger, avoided the last large draft of Page County men just prior to the Battle of New Market in 1864.[12] Instead of being conscripted for the Confederate Army, he left Page County to enlist in a cavalry unit from Pennsylvania. Nevertheless, by war's end,

Emma Jane Shuler. *Courtesy of John and Sandie Hammel.*

the combined communities had lost over twenty men in the Confederate service—most as a result of being killed in action.[13]

One of those men lost in battle was Captain Michael Shuler. As Isaac Shuler later commented, his father, John Shuler, "being opposed to war, but when we got into it, being a loyal man to his home and fireside, he gave one son that yielded his life for the lost cause."[14] At the opening of the war, Shuler was a student at Roanoke College. "The students [there] raised a company, the parents of the students heard about it and ordered them home a month before their term was up. He came home and the country was at war. He could not think of keeping out of it," and joined the ranks of Rippetoe's infantry company—the same company later being attached to the Thirty-third Virginia Infantry as Company H. [15] Just six months after his eighteenth birthday, Michael Shuler found himself in command of the company, in which capacity he remained for the next two years.[16] On May 5, 1864, in action near Saunder's Field at the battle of the Wilderness, Shuler's company stood along with the rest of the old Stonewall Brigade and bore the brunt of a fierce Union assault. Just four months short of his twenty-first birthday, Shuler was killed in that fight.[17]

Though the rest of John Shuler's children were too young to fight, his oldest daughter, Emma Jane, knew well the horrors of war and feared for the life of her fiancé, Sergeant Isaac Newton Koontz. Not only did she lose her brother and several friends from her congregation at Monger's Meeting

George Summers Sr.
Courtesy of Joann Rothgeb Schaub.

House, but early on in the war, on January 15, 1862, her uncle, Captain John D. Aleshire, was killed in a small fight at Hanging Rock near Winchester, Virginia, while in command of Company I of the Ninety-seventh Virginia Militia.[18] However, with war's end, it appeared that the young love that Emma and Newton shared would not be denied—at least it seemed so.

John Shuler would suffer much for the loss of his oldest son and both Shuler and Walton had spoken out against secession; however, Grove Hill resident George Summers would quite possibly suffer the most in the community during the war. Believed the most outspoken advocate for Union in that area of Page County, Summers's life both before and during the war seemed to be plagued with crisis—some as a result of being outspoken, some as a result of war and some simply a part of life and survival in the mid-nineteenth century.[19]

The first traumatic episode of war in the Summers family centered on his second oldest daughter, Mary Summers Strole. By 1862, Hiram and Mary Summers Strole had two daughters, Amanda Susan (born 1857) and Mary Lee Virginia (born 1859).[20] But in 1862, not yet five years old, Amanda died from sickness on January 22. Four days later, her mother Mary followed in death. This left only two-year-old Mary Lee with Hiram as the sole parent. A former first lieutenant of Company L, Ninety-seventh Virginia Militia, despite the loss of his wife and daughter and the prospect of leaving his last daughter as an orphan, Hiram enlisted on March 15, 1862, with Company

Brigadier General John P. Hatch. *Courtesy of* Generals in Blue: Lives of the Union Commanders, *by Ezra J. Warner.*

H, Thirty-third Virginia Infantry. However, knowing the hazards that faced him, Hiram took the precaution of making out his last will and testament, looked after the well-being of his only daughter in the event of his death— leaving all of his "lands and the benefits thereof."

In the months that followed, Hiram braved the elements and battles in the Valley, around Richmond and finally in the fields around Manassas. Though he survived the intensely heated contest at Brawner Farm on August 28, 1862, the following day Hiram was killed. Captain Michael Shuler wrote that after falling "back a short distance, [they] were not able to get the dead off." Ultimately, Hiram's body was recovered and brought back to Page and buried next to his wife and daughter near the Summers family home.[21] Within days of her third birthday on September 3, Mary Strole was an orphan and left to the care of her grandparents.

While tragic enough, the difficulties and heartache in the family were not all of the trials that were to befall George Summers Sr. in 1862. When Union troops moved into and occupied Page County in April, being a devout Union man, Summers was able to secure protection orders for his mercantile stores from Union Brigadier General John P. Hatch. However, and as was typical, after Hatch went on ahead with his command, Union troops who followed up behind had little regard for such orders. In May 1862, General James Shields's army passed along the River Road toward Grove Hill and eventually Port Republic. Despite his loyalty to the Union, Summers's store became subject to pillage. Wrote Summers, "A portion

Major C. Roberdeau Wheat. *Courtesy of* Gentle Tiger: The Gallant Life of Roberdeau Wheat, *by Charles L. Dulfour.*

Brigadier General Robert C. Schenk.
Courtesy of Generals in Blue: Lives of the
Union Commanders, *by Ezra J. Warner.*

of his army camped near my store three or four days. Living on the other side of the river from my store and not anticipating any damages from Shields' Army encamped close by, I went to my house at night as usual. Shields' army passed during my absence and carried off my whole stock of goods and merchandise, which amounted to around one and two thousand dollars when I got to my store in the morning. The house was broken open and everything gone. My papers were strewn along the road towards Port Republic for several miles. I had a general apartment as is usually kept in a country store, Boots, shoes, hats." Apparently, in this same incident, several hundred dollars worth of store notes were stolen by Union soldiers as well. In an effort to prevent the illegal circulation of these notes as legal tender, Summers posted a note on the door of his store:

> *To The Public—It is pretty generay known that a short time ago the Yankyes entered my store and stolen Sum six or Eight Hundred Dollars of my own money to which I had never put my signature I find that said Yankeys are trying to counterfit my name & passing said money on the people the publick will please be upon ther Guard as I will Recive none but those I signed my self George Summers.*

26

When a part of the Fifth New York Cavalry came through, Union cavalry officer William P. Bacon took down the note and scribbled on the same that he did so "before the owner's eyes."[22]

Summers's constant struggle to maintain proof of his loyalty to passing Union commands also placed him in a rather awkward and dangerous position with some people in the community, as well as Confederate soldiers who frequently camped nearby. Local resident John Welfley recalled that, because of Summers's outspokenness regarding his loyalties, he had "Heard a great many parties threaten him with arrest saying that—as he ought to be killed that such men as he caused a great deal of trouble in the army."[23] Such threats were quite sincere as had been seen with the "running-off" of several Union men from Page County, but most especially in the case of the two local Unionists who were executed by a small band of overzealous civilian secessionists in April of 1862.[24]

Grove Hill neighbor Samuel Step had made a similar statement in another affidavit and had "heard men say Summers ought to be hung that he be to stay here I was alarmed for him."[25] Summers himself recollected that, during the time in which General Richard S. Ewell's Confederates camped in the area in late April and early May 1862, Major C. Roberdeau Wheat of the Louisiana Tigers and a Captain White had "told me that if I uttered one word more" regarding Union sympathies, "a thousand men would kill me." Yet he remained "unmolested at times" he felt that his "life was at stake."

Further troubles arose a year later. Summers had felt from the beginning that Confederate money would not hold its value, and thereby partnered with William H. Forrer in the purchase of tobacco in Maryland. Summers and Forrer made several trips to Berlin, Maryland, during the war, and on one trip the partners were arrested by Union soldiers and taken to Baltimore. Brought before Union General Robert C. Schenk, the men explained their situation and, with the assistance of a local attorney (Daniel Miller of the firm of Daniel Miller and Co.) and an extremely heavy bond, they were released. Schenk also issued the two men permits to cross lines as necessary in order to secure supplies for their families and others with Union sympathies. Likewise, and apparently in the same trip, the tobacco was turned over to the men and sold "for greenbacks and bankable Maryland money."[26]

Upon returning to Page, Summers and Forrer were threatened with arrest by Confederate authorities but such arrests did not come to be. "A party of soldiers were sent to me," noted Summers, "but were prevented by the fullness of the river from marching my home. The Confederate Cutthroats took my goods, burnt my rails and____[illegible] upon me as they pleased."

The elder Summers again fell victim to the Federal Army during the horrible period known as the "Burning" of October 1864 when Colonel William H. Powell's Federal cavalry took three horses from Summers's property. After gaining an audience with Powell personally, Summers was given permission to search the camps and have his horses returned. However, Summers not "knowing the full extent of the camp and having no guide I found only two." A six-year-old sorrel could not be located and as Summers later stated, he never "received pay for him."[27]

When the war had finally come to an end and his only son was finally safe at home, Summers's hardships were not yet at an end.

Going Home: Spring 1865

By the middle of May 1865, after four years of war, things finally seemed to be returning to normal in the Page Valley. Several men were still being held in prisoner of war camps in the North, but a good number had already made their way home from the army. Certainly there were those who must have seen the irony in the season. Within a week of the surrender of the Army of Northern Virginia at Appomattox, some of the Valley men would easily make it to church for Easter Sunday services on April 16. Likewise, spring was in the air and with it, a rebirth of the land. Both the music of the songbirds and the blossoming of the trees and of the land must have been welcome replacements for both the cold and depression of the winter and the last months of the Confederacy.

Furthermore, though the "Yankees" had taken a good number of the livestock the previous fall, there were still enough sheep left to begin shearing soon. Not only that, but the new moon on April 25 meant that corn should soon be sown and, in the time that followed, there would soon be fields of hay to mow, rye to harvest, oats to cut and then cane, potatoes and buckwheat to plant.

For what few men remained in the ranks of the Massanutten Rangers, the war came to a close only a day after Appomattox, when Colonel Elijah V. White, commanding the Laurel Brigade, gave the order at Lynchburg, Virginia, to disband. The men of the brigade were at liberty to either accept the terms of surrender or to make an effort to join the army of Joseph E. Johnston, a decision that each man would have to make for himself.

In the four years behind them, the horsemen of Captain George W. Summers's Massanutten Rangers had seen their share of good times

Colonel Elijah V. White. *Courtesy of Library of Congress.*

General Turner Ashby.
Courtesy of Stonewall
Jackson's Way, *by John
W. Wayland.*

and bad. With the financial backing from local county merchant and Luray resident Gabriel Jordan, the Rangers had been Page County's first company of cavalry. By June 1, 1861, the company was mustered into the service of the Commonwealth and the Confederacy at Luray, with Gabriel Jordan's youngest son, Macon, in command. A former student of Jedediah Hotchkiss's Mossy Creek Academy in Augusta County, Macon Jordan brought with him little in the way of experience.[28] Nevertheless, with a full compliment of men, the company was accepted on June 19 into the ranks of Colonel Angus W. McDonald's cavalry command, which subsequently became the Seventh Virginia Cavalry. The Rangers would serve as Company D of that regiment. In time, the Seventh Virginia would come under the command of Colonel Turner Ashby and then, later on, under Thomas L. Rosser, who gave the brigade to which the Seventh was attached the name Laurel Brigade. From the Shenandoah to Upperville, Brandy Station, the Black Water and the famous Beefsteak Raid, and on to the last hours before they broke out from the encirclement at Appomattox, the Seventh had taken part in a considerable number of battles and had seen its fair share of men lost along the way. But, in April of 1865, it was finally time to come home to stay.

Among those of the Massanutten Rangers who had chosen to return home were Captain Summers, Sergeant Isaac Newton Koontz and Privates Andrew Jackson Kite and Jacob Daniel Koontz. All four men had seen extensive service throughout the war. "Jolly Jake" Koontz had been the last to join the Rangers, having enlisted on January 23, 1863, just over a month after his eighteenth birthday. Within three months of having enlisted, Jake Koontz's horse was killed in action at Greenland Gap in Hardy County, Virginia (now West Virginia). Detached for a brief time from March to April 1864, Koontz appears to have been present for the balance of the war. Jake was a first cousin to Sergeant Isaac Newton Koontz and lived less than a quarter of a mile from the Columbia Bridge near Alma in central Page County.[29]

Andrew Jackson "Jack" Kite enlisted on April 20, 1862, a day after the Federal Army had entered Page County and occupied it for the first time. A resident of Grove Hill, Kite was both the oldest and the only married man of the four men—though he had been widowed at some point during the war, leaving him with three young children. Kite was a house joiner by occupation.[30]

Newton Koontz enlisted on April 15, 1862, just days before Union troops entered Page County and first occupied Luray.[31] Having just turned seventeen years old only days before he had enlisted, Koontz was serving as fourth sergeant by the late fall of 1862. Wounded severely in the leg in action at Bottom's Bridge outside of Richmond on August 18, 1864, Koontz appears to have returned to duty by late war.[32] The son of a prosperous farmer, Koontz, like his cousin Jacob D. Koontz, lived on the south side of the South Fork of the Shenandoah River, opposite Alma. The Koontz family had deep roots in Page County, having arrived in the area in the early eighteenth century one generation removed from having settled in Governor Alexander Spotswood's famous Germanna Colony. Descended from a long line of seventeenth- and eighteenth-century Lutheran ministers in both Germany and America, Newton's great-grandfather—Elder John Koontz—broke the mold and had been instrumental, along with one other, in spreading the Baptist faith in the area in the mid- and latter portions of the eighteenth century.

Hiram Jackson Strickler. *Courtesy of Kansas State Historical Society.*

Newton Koontz's return home from the war would surely signal a pleasant event in the near future as, sometime prior to the spring of 1865, he had become engaged to Emma Jane Shuler.

George Washington Summers had been with the Rangers since the very beginning of the war.[33] Summers was also the fourth child and only son of George Summers Sr. and Susannah Hollingsworth Summers, the widow of Abraham Strickler. Interestingly, it was through his stepbrother, Hiram Jackson Strickler, that George W. Summers had interesting connections with the coming of the war. A former student of the Virginia Military Institute, Hiram was dismissed from the Institute because of insubordinate conduct just before graduation.[34] Not long after, he set out for a new life in Shawnee County, Kansas, and soon thereafter became the territory's first (and later third) territorial adjutant general (from August 31, 1855—January 1858 and November 1860—April 16, 1861, respectively). While not involved militarily with troubling affairs in Kansas, he was involved in an administrative role in suppressing John Brown's efforts in that area.

Despite his sentiments against abolitionists such as John Brown, Strickler did not partake in the Civil War. In 1861, he retired from public life and "devoted himself wholly to agricultural pursuits," marrying in November of that same year.

While his stepbrother opted to remain out of the war, on June 1, 1861, George W. Summers, despite his father being "bitterly opposed to it," enlisted in the Massanutten Rangers, which were then forming at Luray. In lieu of enlisting, the elder Summers had proposed that his son "go North to go to school there" and had even purchased him a horse to take him out of what would become an endangered arena of war. However, when the war came, the younger Summers went off to war on the horse that his father had purchased for him. In time, his son sent back the horse for having secured another upon which to ride in the campaigns and engagements to come. The elder Summers later reaffirmed that he had, in fact, furnished his son with "anything as I did when [he was] at home" but did not believe that to qualify him as a Southern sympathizer.

George W. Summers rose quickly in rank, from second sergeant to second lieutenant by April 1862. Later promoted to first lieutenant following the death of Captain Samuel Brown Coyner near Culpeper in September 1863, Summers was placed in charge of his company as well as the command of the fourth squadron of the Seventh Virginia Cavalry for some time. Wounded at the fight at Mechanicsburg Gap in February 1864, upon his return to duty he was officially elected captain of the Massanutten Rangers. He was listed as sick on a surgeon's certificate in

Captain Samuel Brown Coyner. *Courtesy of* Confederate Veteran Magazine, *Vol. 3.*

October 1864, but appears to have returned to duty near the end of 1864 and served for the duration of the war.

Constantly concerned with life and death in the field, George W. Summers was also troubled frequently by events at home—especially when it came to his father's outspoken stand for the Union.

3

The Trouble Begins

Like most of the South's surviving residents, many of the people of the Shenandoah Valley took little pleasure in the continued presence of Union soldiers, most especially as an occupational force. To make matters worse, many Confederate veterans who had escaped capture or surrender faced a difficult reality. Their cause was lost and they were required to take the oath of allegiance. On the morning of May 22, 1865, George W. Summers, Newton Koontz, Jake Koontz and Jack Kite assembled to do just that—since their regiment had been disbanded and they had not themselves surrendered, the time had come to obtain their paroles.[35]

Setting off from Page County early that day, the men rode across the Massanutten and down the Valley Pike toward Woodstock and eventually past a party of Union troops conveying ex-Governor John Letcher out of the Valley. Passing the small caravan without incident, minutes later at or near Narrow Passage, the group came upon a band of about a half-dozen troopers of Company H, Twenty-second New York Cavalry. What took place between the two parties or what words might have been exchanged can only be speculated upon, but in short order the Confederates ended up drawing their revolvers and demanding that the Federals surrender their horses. While the majority of the bluecoat horsemen reluctantly consented, the Union lieutenant with the party resented the demand and drew his pistol.[36] In turn, one of the four Page County Confederates quickly turned his piece toward the gun-wielding lieutenant. In a blink of a moment, both men pulled the triggers, but neither pistol discharged and each produced no more than a "pop" of the caps. Inevitably, the lieutenant surrendered his horse.

Writing about the incident a few months later, the elder George Summers mentioned that "My son stated to me that this whole thing had transpired

Governor John Letcher.
Courtesy of Library of Virginia.

but a few moments before he was truly sorry for what had just happened; and have the thing to have gone over he would have acted very differently. But the act was done—the error committed and a mournful scene does the sequel disclose to poor, sinful man." Apart from admitting that his son and the other men had acted unwisely and the "error committed," why the elder Summers did not give more specifics as to why the Confederates demanded the surrender of the horses leaves a major question for many to ponder.

Well realizing the trouble that could come from the incident, the four men returned to their homes in the Page Valley. After the facts of the incident had been ascertained, Captain Summers's father recalled that "it was truly painful for me to reflect upon the misfortune that the unfortunate boys had fallen into. I at once stated to my son that some evil would grow out of the affair, which would no doubt give him and his parents a great deal of trouble. He thought differently." The elder Summers's "wish and desire was that the property be returned immediately to some of the authorities in the Valley, where a settlement or compromise might be made satisfactory to all parties concerned. Some thought differently and concluded it would lead to their immediate arrest."

The Story of the Summers-Koontz Execution

Considering the execution of Unionists Beylor and Haines, as well as a number of events that resulted in the "running-out" or deadly threats to Unionists in Page County in the first two years of the war, Summers, Kite, Newton and Jake Koontz had good reason to be concerned about being arrested and the possible backlash that would come, despite the fact that they could not have had a part in the deeds that had been done. Activities of "fire-eating secessionists" left a sour taste in the mouths of Union officers as early as April 1862, and Luray very narrowly escaped being burned to the ground that same spring. As the war progressed, the activities of these radicals proved bad for everyone in the county, and as the fortunes of the war turned, scorned Unionists who had weathered the storm and remained in Page County began to take their revenge for earlier wrongs done to them. In recounting the events of the burning in 1864, one local commented of the "home enemy" being far worse than the "foreign enemy."[37]

The next morning, "several respectable citizens employed to go to camp at or near Rude's Hill" and to the camp of the 192nd Ohio Volunteer Infantry. The regiment had only been organized months before at Camp Chase, Ohio, on March 9, 1865, to serve one year. While the regiment did have veterans of other regiments in its ranks, the 192nd Ohio saw no combat service.

The 192nd Ohio was commanded by Colonel Francis Wellington Butterfield, a man recognized by a few early on in the war as of "good moral character and temperate habits."[38] A carpenter or house joiner by profession and a married man, Butterfield had originally joined the army on June 5, 1861, at Camp Davison in Bucyrus, Ohio, and was mustered in as captain of Company C, 8th Ohio Infantry. The 8th Ohio saw extensive service beginning with the 1862 Shenandoah Valley Campaign and later, battles that included South Mountain, Sharpsburg, Fredericksburg, Chancellorsville, Gettysburg, the Wilderness and Petersburg, where it was mustered out on July 13, 1864. During the assault on Marye's Heights at Fredericksburg, one soldier of the 8th Ohio, Thomas Galwey, remembered Butterfield's courage under fire. Galwey noted that during the fight, while the nearby 24th and 28th New Jersey "did not exactly run," they "were very nervous all the time." When two cannon shells burst in the ranks of the Garden State men, terror was immediately thrown into the hearts of the unseasoned soldiers. Seeing this, Butterfield reassured the men, telling them that the Confederates could never land three shots in the same spot. While his words seemed to reestablish the confidence of the New Jersey men, a bystander observed another shell exploding "with a tremendous crash right among them," sending the Jersey men reeling to safety. Butterfield remained with the 8th Ohio for nearly two more years before he was mustered out of service on July 13, 1864, at Cleveland, Ohio.[39]

In relation to this particular episode regarding the young men from Page County, it is interesting to note that as early as August 1861, Butterfield was first familiarized with dealing with enemy civilians. Temporarily detached from his regiment, he was assigned to duty at Cumberland, Maryland, where he was ordered to arrest "rebel citizens."[40] In recalling the meeting with Colonel Butterfield, the elder Summers noted that he "received them very kindly and courteously." After Summers explained his mission to the attentive colonel, Butterfield agreed that the matter was indeed "an unfortunate thing for the boys, but he had no doubt that if the property would be returned there would be a final adjustment of the whole matter." According to Summers, Butterfield continued that "the property could be sent, or the boys could bring it over; that they should not be molested nor disturbed." Accordingly, all of the property was returned, "or nearly so," remarked the elder Summers; "even a dollar and a half in money that had been procured from the soldiers was returned to the Colonel, for which he very politely gave a receipt for all the property returned."

Satisfied that their mission was a success, the four young men and their friends returned home. However, no account was made of the transaction in the Ohio regiment's Morning Order book.

Tharp's Promise of Retribution

Although for the ex-Confederates the matter appeared to be resolved, trouble for the young men again surfaced on Sunday, June 21, when a local Union sympathizer, William Tharp, got into an argument with a former Confederate over an incident during the war.[41] According to an account given by Isaac Shuler in the fall of 1923, "Benjamin and Lewis Kite, Jacob Koontz and a Mr. Tharp were the parties interested."[42] Shuler wrote, "After the war was over, the above men were at the brick church, known as St. Paul's Lutheran church, two miles south of Newport, Page County, attending a singing school. I happened to be on the outside when the trouble started, and I will never forget the remark made by Tharp to Benjamin Kite, a man that had been so loyal to his home and State. He stepped up to Benjamin, denouncing his acts during the war and kept it up from one thing to another. Kite and his brother, Lewis, were sitting on a log. Tharp finally said that every dog has his day. Lewis then arose to his feet and grabbed Tharp and gave him a good shaking and told him the war was over and they wanted to hear no more from him. The noise of the disturbance attracted those inside the church and Jacob Koontz rushed to the door, and asked the cause of the trouble.[43] Whereupon, Tharp said to him, 'Jacob Koontz, you take those horses back you stole.'[44] Jacob raised a brick and if some one would not have then grabbed him, he [Tharp] would never have been able to carry his falsified report to the Yankees at Rude's Hill...Capt. Summers...was sitting behind the church at the time and knew nothing of the affair until it was all over. When told of the affair he shed tears well knowing that this would bring wrath of the Federal host upon him."[45]

Of Tharp's threat, the elder George Summers later recollected, "Now, what was the result of the threat? Tharp started the same day from the

St. Paul's Lutheran Church. *Courtesy of the author.*

meeting house for the camp at Rude's Hill, and no doubt gave a very unfair statement of what had occurred on Sunday, and to my great surprise, and the surprise of the whole community, moved by Tharp, or their own accord, they did come on Monday night according to the threat that was made by Tharp on Sunday."

"Yes, you did go," wrote Summers, "I believe you were the cause of the arrest of my son. I still cannot think you could have desired the evil that occurred to my son. But your course was unjustifiable in running for Yankees to come over for no just cause under the heavens; you can exonerate yourself from the charge preferred if you can. I know my son never treated you unkindly, or spoke one disrespectful word against you."

Whether or not Tharp actually carried out his threat cannot be ascertained due to the lack of information available. There is no record in the logs of the 192nd Ohio of Tharp arriving at the camp and delivering a story about the men. One event worthy of note, however, is that, as of June 16, Colonel Butterfield had gone on furlough and Lieutenant Colonel Cyrus Hussey was left in command.[46] Another known fact is that on Monday, June 26, Special Order #3 was issued by Hussey to Captain Lycurgus D. Lusk, commanding Company H, 22nd New York Cavalry, to "proceed to Luray Valley at 9:00 p.m. and there arrest and execute severally and all without delay whatsoever, the following named men who had been guilty of attacking U.S. troops and stealing horses since the surrender."[47] The four young men were named and underlined several times in red. The order for execution was according to General Order #1 and was also noted in a post-war reference

Captain Lycurgus D. Lusk. *Courtesy of Philip D. Lusk.*

Yours Truly
Cyrus Hussey

Baldwin   Photo. Columbus, O.

Previous page: Lieutenant Colonel Cyrus Hussey. *Courtesy of Stephen E. Williams.*

as having been carried out in accordance under instructions "from Army and Department Headquarters." The following morning, Hussey penciled a letter to Major William Russell Jr. in the adjutant general's office that these four men "constituted the gang that attacked, robbed, and drew arms upon the party of cavalry at the narrow pass below here on or about the 22nd day of last month."[48]

According to a modern biographer, Cyrus Hussey was "a stern and righteous man." However, "he had lost his pacifism but not his self-righteousness [and] that was probably a dangerous combination when he was occupying territory rather than invading it. He apparently never did have a sense of humor."[49]

Born in Highland County, Ohio, on November 4, 1838, Hussey was the second youngest of ten children. Interestingly, Cyrus's father, Stephen, was born in Orange County, North Carolina, in 1793 and only later did the Hussey family migrate to Ohio.[50] A schoolteacher prior to the war, Hussey was married to Rebecca A. Hodson on December 24, 1859. Quaker records show that Rebecca was disowned by the Clear Creek Monthly Meeting for joining the Methodist Episcopal Church in July 1858. Later, in the summer of 1860, Cyrus Hussey was disowned as well for his marriage to Rebecca, who was no longer a Quaker, and for joining the Methodist Episcopal Church himself.[51]

On September 9, 1861, Hussey enlisted in Company A, Forty-eighth Ohio Infantry in New Lexington, Ohio. No doubt, the death of his five-month-old daughter, just three days later, must have had a significant impact on his outlook on life at that time, especially just before his departure from his family.[52]

During his three years with the Forty-eighth O.V.I., he rose from private to captain (February 1863) of Company A. According to his biographer, at this point in time, Hussey held a great deal of suspicion of "anyone who spoke of the Union in a disloyal way." He once refused to sign a recommendation for promotion of a soldier to the rank of second lieutenant because he "had made disloyal statements."[53]

Hussey experienced action first at the battle of Shiloh and was a veteran of the siege of Corinth, Mississippi, the capture of Arkansas Post and the Vicksburg Campaign (the regiment was at Port Gibson and Champion's Hill). In April 1864, Hussey was detached from the Forty-eighth Ohio for temporary duty at the Ohio Draft Rendezvous in Columbus, Ohio. At that same time, most of his regiment ended up being captured during the Red River Expedition.[54]

With the handful of men remaining from the old 48th, the regiment was merged with the 83rd O.V.I. and Hussey was mustered out at Columbus,

Ohio, as a supernumerary officer in December 1864. However, four months later, on April 30, 1865, Hussey was appointed as lieutenant colonel of the newly formed 192nd Ohio Volunteer Infantry. He remained with this regiment until mustered out in September 1865.[55]

The Darkest of Days

Early on the morning of June 27, Captain Lusk's company reached the vicinity of the homes of George Summers and Daniel Koontz and proceeded to encircle them. According to an account given by local Jacob R. Seekford in the *Page News & Courier* in June 1933, that night both Jake Koontz and Isaac Newton Koontz were staying at the Daniel Koontz home. "Old Mr. Koontz got up before day and went out on the porch and heard noises when they [the Federal cavalry] crossed over a bridge [a small bridge that crossed the road not far from the house—not to be mistaken with the old Columbia Bridge that had been burned in June 1862] about two hundred yards away from the house."[56] Mr. Koontz ran upstairs to tell the boys of this, though, according to a later account of the affair, "not knowing what it meant, but he thought that they had better get out of the house and hide." He succeeded in waking his son, Jacob, who jumped out a door with nothing on but his nightclothes, supposedly with Federal troops firing at him as he ran. Seekford continued that Jacob Koontz "made his escape by going into the Massanutton mountain. Mr. Koontz could not get Newton Koontz out of bed and the Union soldiers rode in and arrested him when he was still in bed. When they brought him down the steps, he asked them to let him tell his folks goodbye. When he went to shake the hand of old Mrs. Koontz this old clock began to strike and he said, 'Aunt Betty, tell my sweetheart to remember me when the clock strikes.'"[57]

Able to make his escape, Jake Koontz was said to have climbed a thick cedar tree where he evaded his potential captors. Another account states that he ran up through a nearby hollow and into a forest where he stayed for about a week, his mother bringing him food.[58] Jackson Kite was also

Remains of Daniel Koontz house. *Courtesy of the author.*

Ruins of Columbia Bridge. *Courtesy of the author.*

successful in evading the Federals, though no account of his escape was known to have been published.

Newton Koontz and his captors stopped briefly at Noah Kite's Mill. While there, Koontz apparently saw a familiar passerby and asked the lieutenant in charge of the detail permission to draft a quick note and have the friend dispatch it to his betrothed. The lieutenant allowed it and Newton wrote:

My Dearest girl—

I write to inform you that I was arrested this morning Before day light at Uncle Daniel Koontz's in bed. I am now under arrest. I hope dearest Emma you will bear up under this as well as you can, and doubt not but that God will allow me to return to you. He will not allow such innocence to be bereft of its happiness. I hope Mr. Shuler will take some interest in my welfare and do some thing for me if possible, I expect to be carried to Mount Jackson, where I suppose they will give me an honorable trial. The Lieutenant and men appear to be gentlemen, But Emma I must close these lines, writing will avail nothing I only hope it will comfort you, I am conscious of having acted the part of a gentleman in returning the horses, I have the consolation of knowing I have faced death on a hundred battlefields, and should it be my sad lot to suffer death, I shall endeavor to die a brave man, and a gentleman. Miss Emma I hope you will think of me and remember me in your prayers, my love and regards to your father and mother and family, Forget not one who loves and esteems you dearer than life and think not that I will return no more but consider me yours as ever the same in life or death, May God bless and protect you, is my humble prayer,

Yours,
NEWTON KOONTZ

While Newton Koontz had been taken from the Daniel Koontz home, another portion of the cavalry detail had arrived at the George Summers home. According to Summers, "On the morning of the 27th of June, 1865, there did a party of Federal soldiers, then and on that day, surround my house. I arose from my bed and went and spoke to the two Captains that were in command of the party. I spoke to them kindly and inquired of them what their business was? They informed me that they had come to arrest my son. I inquired by whose authority? They replied the order was from headquarters."

Summers then stated that "If it was on account of those captured horses, that I had hoped that matter was all settled; that we had been to see Col.

Ca. 1910 view of Massanutten Gap, from a Postcard from the Albertype Co., Brooklyn, New York. *Courtesy of the author.*

Butterfield and that he had assured us that if the property would be returned that the matter would terminate in the release of the boys. I stated that the property was all returned and that I had done all that I could do."

Despite Summers's attempt to prevent the arrest, "the Captains remarked that they knew nothing about it and their remarks were in a rough, unpleasant manner to me." However, Summers "had breakfast prepared for the Captains and their men, they eat and drink with me, they sat at the same table with my son and partook of the necessary comforts of life."

At some point during the morning, Captain Summers remarked to his father, "'Papa, I think that I could make my escape.' I replied, no George, you had better not make the attempt. You might fail and it might make the matter worse, you had better go. I want you honorably released. I think there can be no doubt of your release as the property has been returned and we have done all that could be done. I trust in what Col. Butterfield stated, that if the property were returned, that you would get your discharge."

Soon after the party was finished and ready to go, the elder Summers recalled that his son was "still cheerful and hopeful he rising from his seat, said farewell Father, farewell Mother, farewell to my home forever." Though the elder Summers was not able to accompany the squad, he later met up with them at the Koontz house on their way over the mountain. "They stopped a while and were waiting, for what I could not tell. They seemed

Modern view of the Route 211 bridge over Smith Creek, near the base of the Massanutten Mountain, Shenandoah County, Virginia. *Courtesy of the author*

to be unkind to me all the time and gave me no satisfaction whatever. They very coldly informed me that I could procure some of the best citizens and come over the next day; it might aid in securing his release."

The Rochester cavalrymen arrived at the foot of the Massanutten Mountain on the Shenandoah County side sometime that afternoon and Summers and Koontz were told of their fate. Up to this point, no mention had been made by their captors of the requirements of Colonel Hussey's order and the boys pleaded for mercy. Though he was not present, the elder Summers seemed privy to the fact that the boys "wept, they begged, they pleaded, they prayed for pardon and forgiveness. They said they knew they had done wrong, that they had done all they could to adjust the difficulty, had given up all the property; but nothing could avail anything."

The Story of the Summers-Koontz Execution

At that point, somewhere along Smith Creek just east of New Market, Summers and Koontz were "placed in position for execution. They however, at this moment requested that some ministers of the gospel should be sent for, to render some spiritual aid and comfort." A note was apparently sent along to Reverend Socrates Henkel, but no ministers came.[59]

"During this interval," wrote the elder Summers, the two young men "thought of writing home to their friends, which they did do. My son, in the mean time, begged and plead that they might be permitted to be taken to camp, and did partially succeed." Captain Lusk soon thereafter left and "gave the matter of execution into the hands of the Lieutenant, and it was with him that he prevailed.[60] He permitted them to proceed, to the Col., in the camp. They got as far as the foot of Rude's Hill, within a few hundred yards of camp.[61] Here they were met by a body of infantry, who informed them that they were not permitted to go to camp and were to be executed on the spot." Summers and Koontz were permitted to write final letters to loved ones. Summers's note was simple.

> *My Dear Father, Mother, Sisters, and Brothers:*
>
> *Very much to my surprise, we must soon leave this world to try the realities of an unknown one, but I pray to God that he may receive my poor, sinful soul. Would to God that I had died on the battlefield in the defense of my dear native South! But it has been otherwise ordered. I submit to my fate. Pray for me, and try to meet me in heaven. I feel as though my God will forgive my sins. Don't grieve after me, my father, mother, sisters, brother, and friends.*

Newton Koontz wrote his fiancée and parents in two separate letters. To his "Darling Emma," he wrote:

> *Oh, how can I write to you? Affliction is bearing me down! But I will write you a few lines. They are now ready to shoot me. Oh, Emma, dearest in the world to me, how can I leave you but I must. Oh, I have heard you too often say it would kill you to hear of my death. But dearest Emma take this as you can. I will endeavor to die as easy as I can. Emma I have loved you dearer than life its self and feel as if I could die for you were you in my fix. Emma I want you to attend my burying. I wish to be buried with this ring on my finger. Emma, my respect to your father and mother whom I have loved as such, no more, but yours in death, I.N. Koontz.*
>
> *P.S. Try to meet in heaven where I hope to go.*

Reverend Socrates Henkel. *Courtesy of* The Lutheran Church in Virginia, 1717–1962, *by William Edward Eisenberg.*

To his parents he dictated a last note:

> *My Dear Father, Brother, Sisters, Nephews, Niece, Black ones and family:*
>
> *I write to bid you all farewell in this world, hoping to meet you all in a better and happier world. I have been bandaged and tied to be shot, but have sent for Parson Henkel, I feel easier than I did at first, I think God is working a change upon me. Remember dear ones that this world is all a shadow, only a moment in life, and death everlasting. Prepare to meet me in heaven every one of you, I will close. Divide my property among you only consider it though as dust, and lay not the value of your lives on riches. Do not let our deaths grieve you, take it easy. I wish to be buried beside my dear mother. No more, goodbye forever.*
>
> *Your darling,*
> *I.N. Koontz*
> *My love to all my friends.*

Thornton Hamilton Taylor. *Courtesy of Janice Taylor.*

Reverend Henkel did not come, and at 7:30 p.m., the men stood before a firing squad. According to what had been told to the elder Summers sometime after the execution, "My son plead that they might be spared till the next day, until his father could come, for I had promised to be over early the next day. The last resort to save themselves, I was informed, was to give the sign of Mason or Odd Fellows, but no, no! Nothing could save my poor boys from their awful fate."

In recalling what he had heard of the event, former Marksville resident Jacob H. Coffman later wrote to the *Page News & Courier* in the summer of 1933 that a cousin of his, Jane Hurt Weakley, was traveling south along the Valley Pike in the company of local Reverend Thornton H. Taylor in his "one-horse wagon."[62] Taylor himself was on his way home to Page County after having fled Page County in fear of his own life at the beginning of the war, having been an outspoken Union man. Near the time of the execution, the party was stopped near Rude's Hill and witnessed the horrible event. Coffman wrote that the party "came to a camp of Union soldiers" who flagged them down and told them to stop, which they did. Mrs. Weakley "noticed the two men on their knees tied to a stake but had no idea what it really meant until a few minutes passed

Summers-Koontz roadside marker, Rude's Hill. The Summers-Koontz Monument can be seen in the background. *Courtesy of the author*.

Ca. 1967 view of the Andrew Jackson Shuler house, Newton Koontz's boyhood home. *Courtesy of* Old Homes of Page County, Virginia, *by Jennie Ann Kerkhoff*.

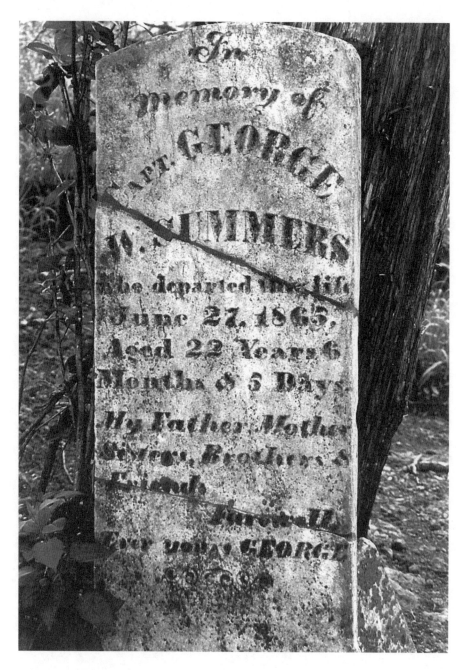

Captain George W. Summers's headstone. *Courtesy of the author.*

Isaac Newton Koontz's headstone. *Courtesy of* Old Homes of Page County, Virginia, *by Jennie Ann Kerkhoff.*

when the shooting was done and seeing the men sink down, she said she fainted. She told me it was the worst thing she had ever witnessed." In the post-war account from the 192nd Ohio Infantry, the conduct of the two men was noted as "exemplary, and very few complaints were made by citizens."[63] Further postwar records of the Buckeye regiment went on to state that "in order to secure the protection of life and property over so large a territory, the punishments for crime were necessarily severe and summary. All offending persons were allowed a trial and counsel, except a party of four guerillas who attacked the forces after the surrender of the Rebels, two of whom, a Rebel Captain and Sergeant, were arrested and summarily executed at Reed's [sic] Hill, June 27th, at sundown."[64] The morning order book of the 192nd Ohio Infantry reads that the execution took place at 7:30, "one mile from camp by musket" and was "conducted by Lt. Henry E. Beeby, Twenty-second New York Volunteer Cavalry, who had relieved Capt. Lusk."

On the morning of June 28, the elder Summers showed up with his friends in order to defend the two men.[65] But before the campsite was reached, and near 11:00 a.m., Summers later wrote that "I came too late, the deed was done…I found my dear, dear George, with his comrade, a lifeless corpse laid on the cold earth with stone for pillows. May the light of day or the rays of sun never, never give light to the like scene again."

On June 29, Captain George W. Summers was laid to rest in the Strickler-Summers family cemetery near Grove Hill, just across the river from Somerville Heights. His stone reads,

In
Memory of
CAPT. GEORGE
W. Summers
Who departed this life
June 27, 1865,
Aged 22 Years, 6
Months & 5 Days.

My Father, Mother,
Sisters, Brothers &
Friends,
Farewell
Ever yours,
GEORGE

Sergeant Isaac Newton Koontz was buried not far from the ruins of the old Columbia Bridge, in the Koontz family cemetery, which was at that time on the Andrew Jackson Shuler farm.[66] Koontz's stone reads,

> *ISAAC NEWTON KOONTZ*
> *Born*
> *April 3, 1845*
> *Killed*
> *June 27, 1865*
> *Aged*
> *20 yrs. 2 mo. 24 days*
> *At the close of the war be-*
> *tween the North and South*
> *this noble young man was*
> *shot by order of Colonel*
> *Hussey, a Northern officer.*

In the Wake of Tragedy

T hough little is known about the details behind it, according to a diary entry made by Reverend Socrates Henkel, perhaps for Sunday, July 2, the minister, upon arriving at St. Paul's Lutheran Church was astounded by what he found following the execution. The entry "tells of a panic the old minister encountered at one of his appointments…where the rumor had spread abroad that the Yankees were coming to butcher all the women and children, causing the male worshippers to appear at the Sunday morning service armed with all sorts of guns and pistols."[67]

Several days later, on Friday, July 7, another party of twenty men under Lieutenant Henry E. Beeby, of Company F, Twenty-second New York Cavalry, set out at 9:00 p.m. pursuant to Special Order 3, Paragraph 1 and Special Order 9 to apprehend and execute Jackson Kite and Jake Koontz.[68] Before the end of the day, however, orders from the headquarters of the Army of the Shenandoah arrived calling for the action to cease. Interestingly, Colonel Butterfield's return from furlough was recorded as July 6, leaving a curious gap in the story as to whether Beeby's party had gone to take Kite and Koontz according to Hussey's orders or not. The two surviving men were pardoned by Union General Alfred T.A. Torbert, who almost a year earlier had executed six of Colonel John S. Mosby's Rangers.[69]

On that same day, the *Rockingham Register* first carried the story of the execution. In the article it stated that Summers and Koontz "were both young men, most respectably connected, and their melancholy fate has caused profound sorrow in the minds of all who knew and who have heard of the circumstances under which their lives were sacrificed." Four days later the same story appeared in the *Staunton Spectator*.

Alfred T.A. Torbert. *Courtesy of* The Photographic History of the Civil War, *edited by Dudley H. Miles.*

The Story of the Summers-Koontz Execution

In the July 28, 1865 issue of the *Rockingham Register and Advertiser*, Colonel F.W. Butterfield, apparently concerned with the impact made by word spread over the Summers-Koontz execution, tried to reassure the local citizenry:

Headquarters, U.S. Forces
Rude's Hill, Va., July 19, 1865

To the Citizens of this and adjoining counties:

Whereas, an erroneous rumor had been put in circulation to the effect that all parties who have been engaged in bushwhacking or other similar actions against Federal forces during the war, are to be hunted down, and when caught, summary punishment inflicted, and that fear to such an alarming extent had been by such rumors engendered as to cause many citizens to leave their homes and flee to the mountains and other places for safety, I take this method of informing all that such rumors are false and without any foundation in fact whatever, and that no citizen will be held accountable or be molested for the above named offenses committed prior to the surrender of Gen. Lee's army; but where parties are guilty of the cold-blooded murder of Union people, or of crimes committed since the surrender of Lee's army, are apprehended, they shall in all cases in future have a fair and impartial trial, and when found guilty be punished as the crime merits, and I do earnestly request that all citizens who are absent from their homes through fear caused by such rumors, return at once without fear of being molested, and further, it should be the duty of every good citizen to go at once and subscribe to the Amnesty Oath, as this is the best credential evidence we have that they have a desire to become peaceful and law abiding citizens.

F.W. Butterfield
Col., 192nd O.V. Infantry
Comd'g. U.S. Forces, Rude's Hill, Va.

No further mention of the incident or the distress to the local community was mentioned in history; however, in closing comments about the darkest episode of his life, George Summers Sr. wrote,

Thus I have been bereft of my son, my only son, he is gone and I never will see him again in the flesh. This calamity has caused poor parents to shed many bitter tears, and we can never forget dear George, till we sleep the

long, last sleep in the peaceful grave by his side. I take the liberty to state in relation to myself, that the sun never shone upon a purer union man than I was. This was known as a general thing during the war. I was a union man from the purest motives—was led by no sinister motives whatsoever. For those views, many taunts and sneers and threats were hurled at me. To those that spoke evil and treated me unkindly I did return many kind acts. Those views of mine were known to the authorities at the time of the arrest of my son. I claim that on that ground they should have dealt more leniently and mercifully with my son.

When it was later mentioned that his son was perhaps a member of a guerilla party during the war and that the execution was justified, Summers wrote, "This charge is positively false, and is set up as a pretext to cover or hide, the shameful deed after committed. Many prisoners were taken by him and his command during the war. He was always kind and merciful to them, for his father taught him—so for the mercy I to others show that mercy may be shown to you. Was it so? No, no, no!"

While certainly the act of the execution of his only son was bad enough, the deception by Federal soldiers to a well-known Union sympathizer was a real betrayal of the faith that Summers had held in the cause that he had believed in, despite the punishing repercussions that came to him for it throughout the war.

Many oral accounts exist over the heartache that the elder Summers must have experienced for the loss of his only son. One account recalled that "old man Summers was so grieved over the mistreatment of his son that he nearly lost his mind." Another recalled that Summers had built a bench, "like you would use at the table" and put it in the cemetery every day and sat on the bench for long periods of time reading the Bible or sometimes falling asleep there. While his wife died in 1871, George Summers did not die until September 26, 1877.[70] The Summers family house was torn down in the early twentieth century and today only the family cemetery remains near the site.

As for the family of Isaac Newton Koontz, little is known of the grief the family endured. Having lost his mother to death in 1852, Sergeant Koontz's father, Isaac Newton Koontz, lived until June 17, 1887—only ten days short of the twenty-third anniversary of the death of his youngest son. In 1868, with the birth of her eighth child, Isaac Newton's sister (and Emma Jane Shuler's aunt by marriage), Julia Ann Koontz Shuler, named her new child in honor of her once would-be sister-in-law, Emma Jane Shuler.[71] The only documented story of the family's reaction to Newton's death was actually seen in the obituary of Harrison W. Koontz, Newton's only full brother. It

John Layton Strole. *Courtesy of John and Sandie Hammel.*

was stated that Newton's death was such a hard blow to Harrison that the incident was one that Harrison never liked to discuss.

According to some accounts, Emma Jane Shuler mourned for over a year. Just short of two years from the date of her fiancé's execution, on June 13, 1867, Emma married John Layton Strole, who was a brother of Hiram P. Strole, brother-in-law to Captain Summers. From 1869 to 1886, seven children—four girls and three boys—were born to the couple.[72] Emma died on July 28, 1912, sixteen months after the death of her husband.[73] Even during her marriage, she was known to have her former fiancé's letter in a frame on the wall in her house. She was also known to have made handwritten copies of the letter.

Two years after the incident, widower Jackson Kite married again, this time to Rebecca J. Morris, a daughter of Pleasant and Susan Morris of Greene County, Virginia. With Rebecca, Andrew had two more children, William F. (1868) and Charles P. (1870). Andrew Jackson Kite died on February 7, 1909.[74]

John and Emma Shuler Strole home, ca. 1892. *Courtesy of* The Christian Strole History, *by Kathryn Foltz Layman.*

The Story of the Summers-Koontz Execution

Jacob Daniel Koontz. In a bit of irony and humor, note the U.S. flag in the background, the fish that he is holding and the fact that he was "one of the two fish that got away." *Courtesy of Janet Koontz Robinson.*

Ca. 1880s photo of Cyrus Hussey. *Courtesy of* Portraits of Companions of the Commandery of the State of Ohio, Military Order of the Loyal Legion of the United States.

67

Nearly ten years after the Summers-Koontz incident, Jake Koontz married Bettie Lee Snyder on January 21, 1875.[75] The couple had at least four children by 1888. After having made a living in farming for nearly forty years, Jacob was paralyzed by a stroke around 1901. Three years later, he suffered a recurrence and died three days later at his home near Alma on the afternoon of January 22, 1904.[76] In the same year as his father's death, Frank Lester Koontz, Jacob Koontz's oldest son, joined a local Sons of Confederate Veterans Camp that organized in Luray late that summer; the camp had been named for Captain Summers and Sergeant Koontz.[77]

In years after the war, Colonel Francis Butterfield moved to Missouri, where he settled down in Kansas City. Though the reasons and date of event are unclear, Butterfield also appears to have been brevetted as a brigadier general and later a major general. Often referred to as "general" in the latter part of his life, he apparently lived anything but such a life in his later years. Butterfield in fact continued to make only a modest income as a house joiner, in addition to the twenty-four dollars a month he received from his army pension. By 1883, the accidental wound he had received in 1861 had nearly caused the entire loss of the use of his right hand, "entirely disabling him from working for a livelihood at the business he learned vis—house joiner; that as he grows older the sense of feeling, or touch, grows less." He died of complications from diabetes at Excelsior Springs, Missouri, on June 18, 1894. He left a widow, two sons and a daughter.[78]

Captain Lycurgus Lusk, the officer tasked with executing Summers and Koontz but evading that responsibility, returned to farming after the war and married Augusta A. Sickles in Elsie, Clinton County, Michigan, on April 11, 1866. They later moved to St. Johns, Clinton County, just north of Lansing. The couple had two sons and three daughters. Lycurgus Lusk died on September 2, 1897.[79]

Cyrus Hussey was mustered out of the service for the second time on September 1, 1865, at Winchester. Immediately following the war, from 1865–73, he was attached to the adjutant general's office in Columbus, Ohio, and served as a bookkeeper for Brooks and Hayden, wholesale grocers. During this time, in 1870, Hussey also lost his first wife to consumption. In 1873, Hussey moved to Toledo and served as a bookkeeper for Osborn, Chase and Swayne. Three years later, on June 1, 1876, he married Frances Elizabeth Whittlesey and had two sons: James Whittlesey Hussey and Arthur Duncan Hussey.[80]

In 1885, Hussey found another line of employment as secretary and treasurer of the Toledo Moulding Company. In 1900 he was a fire insurance agent with Whittlesey and Hussey. Nearly seventy years old, Hussey was serving as an agent for the Aerie Insurance Company in Toledo, Ohio, when he applied for his veteran's pension in 1904. Despite surviving war and disease and the trials of time, at nearly eighty-eight years of age, the former officer responsible for the execution of two Page County men was involved in an automobile accident on September 21, 1926, and, suffering from a concussion, died on October 3, 1926. The death certificate attributed senility as a contributory cause of death. Of all of the people directly involved in the Summers-Koontz incident, Cyrus Hussey was the last to die.[81]

The Enduring Legacy of Summers and Koontz

The first real efforts at commemorating the Summers-Koontz execution took place twenty-eight years later when Confederate veteran Thomas Jackson Adams of Quicksburg, Shenandoah County, Virginia, took steps at marking the site of the tragedy.

Adams, a native of Frederick County, was a former member of Company K, Twenty-third Virginia Cavalry, postwar postmaster of Quicksburg and member of the Turner Ashby Camp, United Confederate Veterans. An important fundraiser for several monuments in the Shenandoah Valley, Adams had hoped that the site at Rude's Hill would be "often visited by those who admire courage and fortitude, and the tragic deaths of Capt. Summers and Sergt. Koontz will long live in the memories of our citizens and deserve to be recited in song and story—to show what atrocities our people suffered in war, and how heroically these men met their untimely fate."

The proposed marble monument represented "a cost of about $175, at a low estimate" and was to replace the wooden pillar that had been erected on the spot soon after the execution of the men in 1865.[82] Adams's one-ton marker was constructed of five pieces and made of Italian marble. The base is twenty-eight-by-twenty-eight inches and six inches in height, with a plinth that is twenty-two-by-twenty-two inches and eight inches in height. The die is sixteen-by-sixteen inches and nineteen inches in height and bears different inscriptions on its east, north and south faces. The lettering was done by Mr. Walter M. Cox of Quicksburg, whose father was also a Confederate soldier. The die is surmounted by a column thirty inches in circumference and five and a half feet in height, terminating in a cone. The entire structure is surrounded by the original iron fence, consisting of four posts of solid iron three inches square, sunk deep into the ground, connected with eight

Summers-Koontz Monument, Rude's Hill. *Courtesy of the author.*

rods bolted together. The ironwork was done by Mr. John H. Myers, also of Quicksburg. Henkel & Co. Publishers of New Market provided the complimentary printing for the programs for the dedication.

Contributors to the 1893 monument included several Confederate veterans. From the Seventh Virginia Cavalry were: Colonel Richard H. Dulaney ($25), Erasmus Nicewarner ($1), William H. Olinger ($1), William A. Pence ($1.50), Lieutenant John H. Connel ($5), Benjamin D. Guice ($1) (both Connel and Guice were of Captain Summers's Company D); First Virginia Cavalry: Thomas L. Williamson ($1); Tenth Virginia Infantry: Philip W. Magruder ($5); Twelfth Virginia Cavalry: John T. Colston ($5), Henry W. Glaize ($5), Alonzo F. Grandstaff ($2), R.M. Lantz ($2), John C. Ruby ($1), O. Shirley ($2); Eighteenth Virginia Cavalry: Dr. Isaac N. Baker ($5); Twenty-third Virginia Cavalry: Colonel Charles T. O'Ferrall ($10), Captain Thomas J. Adams ($25), Isaiah Bowman ($1), John E. Hopkins ($1); Captain Rice's Eighth Star Artillery: George W. Koontz ($5), Captain Berryman Z. Price ($8), Jacob H. Woods ($1); Stonewall Brigade: William E. Russell ($1); civilians: M. Bantz ($1), John W. Clinedinst ($1), Miss Sallie Glaize ($1), David Kingree ($1), Gideon Koiner ($.50), Mag Moore ($2), David & Cass Moyers ($1), Miss Nannie Quick ($2), Jacob W. Rice ($1), Noah W. Shuler ($5—also a nephew of Sergeant Isaac N. Koontz), Charles B. Stiegel ($1) and the Honorable M.L. Walton ($5).

The following assisted in erecting the monument: "Mac Loker, Erasmus Nicewarner, Milton Neff, John Sisler, Edward Knott, Gilbert Silvious, John N. Baker, T.J. Adams, Walter N. Cox, John Fox, John Newman, J.W. Kagey's sons, Lemuel Olinger, Ambrose Biller; and John H. Moyers, T.J. Adams, David Moyers, at the fence."[83]

Three years after the unveiling of the Summers-Koontz Monument at Rude's Hill, the George W. Summers Camp No. 68, Grand Camp of Confederate Veterans of Virginia was organized in Shenandoah, Page County, Virginia, and was chartered in 1896 with Robert S. Pritchett (1846–1924) as commander and James E. Price (1844–1897) as adjutant. In 1897 the Summers Camp submitted dues for what appears to have been approximately forty-four members. Leadership also shifted in that same year to Commander Gilbert Talbot Israel (ca. 1840–1900) and Adjutant Thomas A. Miller (1837–1910).[84] The camp sent two delegates to the convention that year: Commander Israel and David W. Wyant (1839–1922).[85] The year 1907 was apparently the last that the G.W. Summers Camp paid dues, though they remained on the books of the Grand Camps organization through 1909.

Another camp to bear the names of the men who were executed was the Summers-Koontz Camp No. 490, Sons of Confederate Veterans (SCV).

This camp was organized with the assistance of Confederate Veterans in another camp in Page County known as the Rosser-Gibbons Camp No. 89, Grand Camp of Confederate Veterans of Virginia. Camp No. 89 had been organized in Luray on April 30, 1898. As with most Confederate Veterans camps in Virginia, the Rosser-Gibbons Camp held dual charters: one with the Grand Camp of Confederate Veterans of Virginia and another, as Camp No. 1561, with the national organization known as the United Confederate Veterans. Chartered as Camp No. 1561 on May 24, 1904, the camp assisted the Sons in organizing their camp by August 4, 1904. The Summers-Koontz Camp was subsequently chartered on September 14 of that same year with Frederick Taylor Amiss (1868–1942), commander; William Kerfoot Adams (1868–1931), first lieutenant commander; Robert Lee McKim (1876–1961), second lieutenant commander; Arthur Ashby Grove (1883–1940), adjutant; William H. Wright (ca. 1886–?), color sergeant; Reverend George Shelby Kennard (1858–1936), chaplain; Julian Shepard Price (1874–1953), treasurer; Dr. H.T. Willis, surgeon; Hugh W.D. Cary (1868–1939), quartermaster; and John Heiskell Booton (1874–1960), historian. Though not a camp officer, the only other known charter member of the camp was Frank Lester Koontz (1877–1945), son of Private Jacob "Jolly Jake" D. Koontz.[86]

Significant projects of the camp included tending to the needs of the aging veterans, helping to organize reunions, collecting the names of all of the county's Confederate Veterans and aiding directly in the fundraising campaign to erect a monument to honor Page County's Confederate Veterans. This particular monument was finally erected in the midst of World War I in 1918 and stands today near the post office in Luray, Virginia. The day the monument was unveiled, the former Summers-Koontz Camp adjutant, Arthur Ashby Grove, was in the trenches of France as a first lieutenant in the Twenty-ninth Infantry Division.

As the ranks of the Confederate Veterans of Page County slowly thinned over the years, with only three members in attendance at the regular camp meeting on May 5, 1928, the Rosser-Gibbons Camp was officially disbanded. Likewise, by 1931, the Summers-Koontz Camp had declined in membership numbers, falling below the requisite number to maintain a charter, and was subsequently disbanded.

In 1998—sixty-seven years after the Summers-Koontz Camp disbanded—another group of individuals, realizing the importance of the Summers-Koontz incident in local history, began to take measures to erect a marker in Page County to honor the men. At a cost of $1,100 it seemed reasonable to erect a Virginia Department of Historical Resources roadside marker. With the goal met by the spring of 1999, the group gave further consideration to

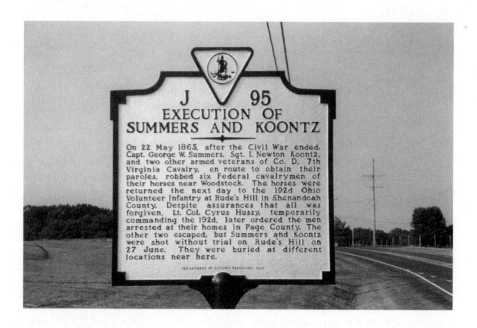

J 95
EXECUTION OF
SUMMERS AND KOONTZ

On 22 May 1865, after the Civil War ended, Capt. George W. Summers, Sgt. I. Newton Koontz, and two other armed veterans of Co. D, 7th Virginia Cavalry, en route to obtain their paroles, robbed six Federal cavalrymen of their horses near Woodstock. The horses were returned the next day to the 192d Ohio Volunteer Infantry at Rude's Hill in Shenandoah County. Despite assurances that all was forgiven, Lt. Col. Cyrus Hussy, temporarily commanding the 192d, later ordered the men arrested at their homes in Page County. The other two escaped, but Summers and Koontz were shot without trial on Rude's Hill on 27 June. They were buried at different locations near here.

Summers-Koontz roadside marker at Page County High School. *Courtesy of the author.*

where the marker should be located and agreed that it would be appropriate to have it placed nearly equidistant in miles between the graves of Captain Summers and Sergeant Koontz, near the sports fields of Page County High School on Route 340. Ironically, at the same time, another effort was being made for placement of a similar marker at Rude's Hill in Shenandoah County by longtime SCV member Davis Coiner Rosen (1928–2004) of New Market.[87] Neither of the two parties working in Page and Shenandoah Counties was ever aware of the other's efforts until the markers were within months of being placed. Both markers were officially dedicated on June 27, 1999, the 134th anniversary of the tragic event.

Later on December 14, 1999, with seven charter members, the Summers-Koontz Camp No. 490, Sons of Confederate Veterans was officially re-chartered and is still active in the community today in monument and cemetery preservation, spearheading funding for Civil War historic markers throughout Page County and many other activities, including an annual overnight vigil held at the Summers family cemetery in Grove Hill over the last weekend in June.[88]

In the hopes of seeing the Summers-Koontz Monument site preserved, on behalf of the Summers-Koontz Camp, early in 2003 camp commander Robert H. Moore II introduced Shenandoah Valley Battlefields Foundation

The Story of the Summers-Koontz Execution

Executive Director Howard Kittell to the landowner of the Shenandoah County property. Situated on the north side of Rude's Hill, the land was of interest to the foundation because it was a part of the critical or "core" battlefield area that related to the May 15, 1864, battle of New Market. In the closing hours of the battle, in an effort to save the bulk of Union General Franz Sigel's army, Union artillery Captain Henry A. DuPont placed his artillery battery at Rude's Hill and successfully delayed the Confederate pursuit. Though the Shenandoah Valley Battlefields Foundation was primarily interested in the land more for its connection with that battle, the ten acres also encompassed the site where Summers and Koontz were executed on June 27, 1865. After two years of working through the details, the land was officially brought under protection by the foundation when they purchased it in March 2005.

Appendix A

Complete Text of "A Fair, Candid and Unbiased Statement of the cause which led to the execution of my Son, Capt. Geo. W. Summers and the circumstances connected therewith. Grove Hill, Page Co., Va., July 24, 1865."

Nearly three months ago, my son, with three other boys, left their homes, as I understood, and were going somewhere to get their parole. Their journey led them across the Massanutten mountain, into the Valley leading from Winchester to Staunton, and while in the Valley near Woodstock, they met a guard of union troops conveying ex-Gov. Letcher down the Valley. After passing the main body some mile or to, at or near the Narrow Passage, they met some half-dozen straggling soldiers, and demanded them to surrender their horses, and with but little resistance, they gave up their horses. One of them however, a Lieutenant, refused to give up his horse, and one of the men that was with my son and the Lieutenant had some difficulty before he consented to surrender his horse. It is fair to state that while this difficulty was going on between the two men, each one presented a pistol at the other, and strange to say, each cap bursted without discharging the contents. The Lieutenant was compelled to give up his horse, and unfortunate boys returned to their houses with their captured property. My son stated to me that this whole thing had transpired but a few moments before he was truly sorry for what had just happened; and had the thing to have gone over he would have acted very differently. But the act was done—the error committed and a mournful scene does the sequel disclose to poor, sinful man.

When I was fully apprised of what had transpired in relation to the capture of the above property, and the circumstances connected with the same, it was truly painful for me to reflect upon the misfortune that the unfortunate boys had fallen into. I at once stated to my son that some evil would grow out of this affair, which would no doubt give him and his parents a great deal of trouble. He thought differently. My wish and desire was that the property be returned immediately to some of the authorities in the Valley, where a settlement or compromise might be made satisfactorily to all parties concerned. Some thought differently and concluded it would lead to their immediate arrest. The effort was however made to adjust the matter and several very respectable citizens employed to go to the camp at or near Rude's Hill, where they found Col. Butterfield in command of the post at that place. They approached the Colonel, who received them very kindly and courteously. They revealed to him their mission: the Colonel heard the whole statement and remarked that was an unfortunate thing for the boys, but he had no doubt that if the property would be returned there would be a final adjustment of the whole matter. The Colonel further remarked that the property could be sent, or the boys could bring it over; that they should not be molested nor disturbed. All was returned or pretty nearly so, even a dollar and a half in money that had been procured from the soldiers was also returned to the Colonel, for which he very politely gave a receipt for all the property returned.

Thus I had fully concluded that the whole matter would be at an end, and so did the poor unfortunate boys; and I still think that the matter would have rested forever, but for a circumstance that occurred in the neighborhood. The circumstance was this: On Sunday previous to their arrest [more than a month following the incident], *at church there was a difficulty between Wm. Tharp and some other party, that had passed between them during the war. Nothing in relation to the matter that claims my immediate subject. Tharp became very much enraged, and one of the boys alluded to above, happened to make a remark of some sort to Tharp, when he (Tharp) exclaimed, "You have better return those stolen horses which were obtained from the Yankees." The young man thanked him, and remarked that he had already returned said horses, and raised something, as though he intended to strike Tharp. During all this difficulty, my son and two of the other boys had nothing in the world to do with the difficulty—said nothing and did nothing. Tharp on the spot exclaimed that he would go to the Yankee camp and get revenge by bringing a squad of Yankees over to arrest the whole party. Now, what was the result of the threat? Tharp started the same day from the meeting house for the camp at Rude's Hill, and no doubt gave a very unfair statement of what had occurred on Sunday, and to my great surprise, and to the surprise of the whole community, moved by Tharp, on their own accord, they did come on Monday night according to the threat that was made by Tharp on Sunday. Yes, you did go. I believe you were the cause of the arrest of my son. I still cannot think you could have desired the evil that occurred to my son. But your course was unjustifiable in running for Yankees to come over for no just cause under the heavens; you can exonerate yourself from the charge preferred if you can. I know my son never treated you unkindly, or spoke one disrespectful word against you.*

Well, the sad story is just beginning to be told. On the morning of 27th of June, 1865, there did a party of Federal soldiers, then and on that day, surround my house, enter it and did arrest my son. I arose from my bed and went and spoke to the two Captains that were in command of the party. I spoke to them kindly and inquired of them what there business was. They informed me that they had come to arrest my son. I inquired by whose authority? They replied the order was from headquarters. I then stated if it was on account of those captured horses, that I had hoped that matter was all settled; that we had been to see Col. Butterfield and that he had assured us that if the property would be returned that the matter would terminate in the release of the boys. I stated that the property was all returned and that I had done all that I could do. The Captains remarked that they knew nothing about it and their remarks were in rough, unpleasant manner to me. I had breakfast prepared for the Captains and their men, they eat and drink with me, they sat at the same table with my son and partook of the necessary comforts of life. Little did myself or son think that they were to be the party that would send the fatal dart to his heart, and cause life's blood to flow free as water, and that by the going down of the sun of the same day. Yes, that was the fate of my dear George. He rose from his bed that morning for the last time—sat at the table and partook of the comforts prepared by the hands of his dear mother for the last time—walked backwards and forwards through the house and porch for the last time. He still seemed to be hopeful and at one time during the morning he remarked to me, Papa, I think that I could make my escape. I replied, no George, you had better not make the attempt. You might fail and it might make the matter worse, you had better go. *I want you honorably released. I think there can be no doubt of your release as the property has been returned and we have done all that could be done. I trust in what Col. Butterfield stated, that if the property were returned, that you would get your discharge.*

But, O, how much I was disappointed! Little did I know or think that I was urging my poor boy from home to be executed by the going down of the sun, whose rays were to shine upon him for the last time. Yes, the word was given, we are ready now to go. Still cheerful and hopeful he rising from his seat, said farewell Father, farewell Mother, farewell to my home forever. They bear him onward, he is gone and the last together with a smile as he used to do.

I met him at Mr. Coontz's on his way over the mountain. They stopped a while and were waiting, for what I could not tell. They seemed to be unkind to me all the time and gave me no satisfaction whatever. They very coldly informed me that I could procure some of the best citizens and come over the next day; it might aid in securing his release. Some friends had made arrangements to go with poor George across the mountain, but by telling us that we should come over the next day they cheated me out of my son, by that unfair and unreasonable statement. The time came and they all got ready to leave Mr. Coontz's. My dear George, my only son for the last time here got upon his horse and when he started off the last word he ever spoke to me was good-bye papa. My last to my dear son was good-bye George. A sad good-bye for me, parted forever, no more to see his face living. O how much was I deceived. O what a deep sting this act has sent into my heart, never to be removed until I close my eyes in the same long dreamless sleep that my son is now sleeping.

When the party reached the foot of the mountain on the other side, here it was that they halted and informed the poor boys of their fate. Here it was they were told that they must die. They no doubt were hopeful to the last, but they now beheld their said, unfortunate fate. Oh! swift as lightning did their thoughts fly back to their loved homes, to Father, Mother, sister, others and friends. Millions they would have given if they could only once more have seen their dear parents, kindred and friends, and have been freed from the cruel hands that held them in confinement their last day. They wept, they begged, they pleaded, they prayed for pardon and forgiveness. They said they knew they had done wrong, that they had done all they could to adjust the difficulty, had given up all the property; but nothing would or could avail anything. They were then placed in a position for execution. They however, at this moment requested that some ministers of the gospel should be sent for, to render them some spiritual aid and comfort. Someone did go to New-market, but none could be procured. During this interval they thought of writing home to their friends, which they did do. My son, in the mean time, begged and plead that they might be permitted to be taken to camp, and did partially succeed. The Captain or Captains that were in command, I was informed, left and gave the matter of execution into the hands of the Lieutenant, and it was with him he prevailed. He permitted them to proceed, to the Col. in the camp. They got as far as the foot of Rude's hill, within a few hundred yards of camp. Here they were met by a body of infantry, who informed them that they were not permitted to go to camp and were to be executed on the spot. My son again plead that they might be spared till the next day, until his father could come, for I had promised to be over early the next day. The last resort to save themselves, I was informed, was to give the signs of Mason or Odd Fellow, but no, no! Nothing could save the poor boys from their awful fate. They yielded at last to their fate and knelt to the stake. They were then and there shot to death, the very same day they were arrested. O shame, where is thy blush. No mercy, no prayer, no trial!

Farewell my dear George—you and your comrade. I trust that our kind heavenly Father, while no one would help or have compassion, that he sustained you in your last, dying moments, and with a look of compassion, pitied you, and sent some ministering angel to bear your spirits to the better clime of an eternal day, where you are done forever with the strife and troubles of this sinful world.

Your last words were, don't grieve after me. Yes, dear George, your parents can't help mourning and grieving after you. Their cup of sorrow is full, and we are drinking its bitter dregs. Your unfortunate end will bring our gray hairs with sorrow to the grave. But our short race on earth will soon be run, and then I hope while our mortal bodies are resting together in their mother dust, we will meet you again. With Cassa, Hiram, little Manda, and all our dear relatives that have gone before us.

You need not tell me, that my son could not have escaped his dreadful end. No, I believe if Col. Butterfield had been at camp at Rude's Hill, when he was arrested, he would be living this day, and moreover, I believe that had the party that executed him, spared him twenty-four hours, so that I could have seen Gen. Tolbert at Winchester, that he would have spared my son. He did reprieve and release the other two boys. I am as certain as I live, that he would have saved my son, if only I could have had the opportunity to have spoken to him. I could, O, I know that I could have prevailed. I pity the party, that not one could be found to have one spark of mercy. The fault lies somewhere with those who had him in their power. A remorse of conscience must fasten itself on some one or other. But, if you had only saved him my gratification would have flowed toward you like rivers that never run dry, and you might, the balance of your days have had great reason to rejoice that you rescued two poor boys from the jaws of death. But none could be found to extend the time a few hours, or to pity or forgive.

I arrived at Rude's hill about 10 or 11 o'clock. I came too late, the deed was done. I found my dear, dear George with his comrade, a lifeless corpse, laid on the cold earth with a stone for their pillows. May the light of day or the rays of the sun never, never give light to the like scene again. Thus I have been bereft of my son, my only son, he is gone and I never will see him again in the flesh. This calamity has caused his poor parents to shed many bitter tears, and we can never forget dear George, till we sleep together the long, last sleep in the peaceful grave by his side.

I take the liberty to state in relation to myself, that the sun never shone upon a purer union man than I was. This was known as a general thing during the war. I was a union man from the purest motives—was led by no sinister motives whatever. For those views, many taunts and sneers and threats were hurled at me. To those that spoke evil and treated me unkindly, I did return good for evil, and to my enemies did do many kind acts. Those views of mine were known to the authorities at the time of the arrest of my son. I claim that on that ground they should have dealt more leniently and mercifully with my son.

My son entered the Confederate service at the beginning of the war as a Sergeant. He was soon after promoted to Lieutenant, then to Captain, and towards the close of the war he was entrusted with the command of a Regiment, which post he held till the surrender of Gen. Lee. He was 22 years, 6 months and 5 days old.

P.S. I have just been informed by good authority that to justify the rash act of the execution of my son, was that he should have belonged to a guerilla party during the war. This charge is positively false, and is set up as a pretext to cover or hide, the shameful deed after committed. Many prisoners were taken by him and his command during the war. He was always kind and merciful to them, for his father taught him—so for the mercy I to others show, that mercy may be shown to you. Was it so? No, no, no!

The following is what he wrote just before he was executed—

BEAR ON, BEAR BRAVELY ON!

O never from thy tempted heart,
Let thy integrity depart;
When disappointment fills thy cup,
Undaunted nobly drink it up;
Truth will prevail, and justice show
Her tardy honors, sure, though slow;
Bear on, bear bravely on.

Bear on! our life is not a dream
Though often such its mazes seem.
We were not born to lives of ease,
Ourselves alone to aid and please;
Bear on, bear bravely on.

Oh! Cast thou not
Affection from thee, in this bitter world!
Hold to my heart that only treasure fast;
Watch—guard it—suffer not a breath to dim
The bright gems of its purity!

'Twere better to have loved and lost,
Than never loved at all!

****

Better trust all and be deceived,
And weep that trust and that deceiving,
Than doubt one heart, which, if believed,
Had blessed one's life with true believing.

Geo. W. Summers,
Capt., commanding Co. D, 7th Va. Cavalry

****

Near New Market, June 27th, 1865.

My Dear Father, Mother, Sisters and Brothers:

Very much to my surprise, we must soon leave this world to try the realities of an unknown one. But I pray God that he may receive my poor sinful soul. Would to God that I had died upon the battle field, in defence of my dear native South; but it had been otherwise ordered; I submit to my fate. Pray for me, and try to meet me in heaven. I feel as though my God will forgive my sins. Don't grieve after me.

Farewell, my Father, Mother, Sisters, Brothers and friends.

Ever yours,

George

The Story of the Summers-Koontz Execution

Lines Composed to the Memory of George. By His Father

You live within a brighter sphere,
And walk the golden streets above;
Your happy spirit with the blest,
Basks in the sunshine of God's love.
Then sleep, dear Captain, calmly sleep,
From all earth's cankering sorrows free;
We would not wish to break the spell,
That binds thee to eternity.

Yes, sleep where violets smile and weep,
And cast at morn each pearly tear,
Where blushing roses softly shed
Their faded leaflets o'er they bier.

And at thy grave by early morn,
When nature bids each flower bloom,
We'll wander in some quiet hour,
And drop a tear upon they womb.

Farewell, dear George, we have resigned
Thy mortal form to earth's cold breast,
Until th' Arch-Angel bids thee to rise
From this thy peaceful, slumbering rest.

Notes

"A Voice from the Ground"

1. Cornelia Jane Matthews Jordan, *Echoes from the Cannon* (Buffalo, NY: Charles Wells Moulton, 1899), 78. This poem was written on May 8, 1885, in preparation for the May 11 Decoration Day events at the Soldiers' Cemetery in Lynchburg, Virginia. Cornelia Jane Matthews Jordan (1830–1898) was a popular Confederate poetess and the wife of Captain Francis Hubert Jordan (1821–1896) of Luray. Captain Jordan served on General P.G.T. Beauregard's staff and was a son of Gabriel Jordan (1793–1862), who was responsible for helping to supply the Massanutten Rangers when they organized in Luray in 1861. F.H. Jordan Sr. was also the brother of Macon Jordan (1841–1908), first captain of the company, and, through his first marriage with Mary Overall Yager (1825–1849), the father of Francis Hubert Jordan Jr. (1845–1888), a corporal in the Rangers.

Chapter 1

2. Population Schedules for the Eighth Census of the United States, 1860, for Page County, Virginia, National Archives, Washington, D.C. According to the 1860 census, Page County had a total of 489 farms valued at $2,192,549, which included 58,431 acres of improved land and 63,600 acres of unimproved acreage. Though the average farm (there were approximately 246 farms in all) in Page consisted of between 100 and 499 acres, 138 farms were between 50 and 99 acres; 80 were 20 to 49 acres; 19 were 10 to 19 acres; 4 were 500 to 999 acres; 1 was 1,000

or more acres; and one was between 3 and 9 acres. Exact figures about how much grain was produced was not disclosed in the 1860 census, but grains known to have been produced during that time included Indian corn, wheat, rye, oats and buckwheat. Additionally, the total value of livestock was $288,509 while orchard products made up only $9,982.

3. Ibid. The households in Alma District 1 alone were listed forty-three farmers, twenty-seven laborers, four colliers, four shoemakers, three blacksmiths, two millers, three merchants, two wagon makers and one each of the following: boatman, cabinetmaker, carpenter, cooper, distiller, iron master, joiner, keeper at the furnace, machine builder, mail carrier, millwright, miner, plasterer, potter, saddler, tailor, tanner, teacher, trader and stonemason.

4. Ibid. Out of the forty-three farms, only nine appear to have utilized slave labor. Though not all were listed as heads of families, individually there were actually twelve slave owners in Alma District 1. David Moncell Dovel (1819–1871) owned the most slaves (thirteen); Noah Foltz (1815–1900, a noted Unionist during the war) ranked next with five slaves; followed by three each for Isaac Koontz Sr. (1810–1887, father of Sergeant Isaac Newton Koontz) and David B. Koontz Sr. (1801–1875).

5. Ibid. In Grove Hill there were twenty-four farmers, thirteen laborers, three joiners, three farmer/millers, two blacksmiths, two boatmen, two carpenters, two coopers, two millers, two shoemakers, one cabinet maker, one farmhand, one farmer/merchant and one wagon maker.

6. Ibid; Slave Schedules for Page County, Virginia, 1860, National Archives, Washington, D.C. Just over a fifth of the farms in Grove Hill had slave labor. James Kite, James J. Kite and Reuben Kite each owned five slaves; Jacob Strole (1789–1860) owned three slaves; George Shuler (1794–1878), father of the John Shuler mentioned in this volume as an outspoken dissenter against secession, owned one slave.

7. *Page News & Courier*. February 11, 1936. John Shuler (1815–1908) was the oldest son of George and Talitha B. Dovel Shuler (1795–1857). He married Mary Ann Kite (1820–1897) on November 22, 1838; she was the daughter of John (1787–1855) and Delia Armentrout Kite (1801–1857).

8. *Page News & Courier*, August 14, 1936. New York-born Peter Bouck Borst (1826–1882) was a prominent lawyer and resident of Luray, District 3 with $40,000 in real estate. A few years after relocating to Luray, Borst married Isabella C. Almond, daughter of Mann Almond (1796–1883), a prominent merchant and Luray slaveholder (owning seven slaves in 1850 and five slaves in 1860). Benjamin Franklin Grayson (1815–1893) was sheriff and a resident of Luray, District 3 with $1,450

in real estate. Martin Strickler (1837–1925) was a farmer and resident of Alma, District 1. He was living with his parents, David and Polly Strickler. While Martin was not listed with any real estate, his father, who was also a farmer, was listed with $10,500 in real estate. John Dofflemoyer (ca. 1810–?) was a farmer and resident of Grove Hill District 1 with $3,400 in real estate. Out of the four men mentioned as pro-secessionist, two (Borst and Grayson) were listed as slaveholders in 1860 (Borst owning one slave and having one hire on his property; Grayson owning two and having one hire). Strickler and Dofflemoyer were not listed as slaveholders in either 1850 or 1860, though Strickler's father was listed as owning one.

9. Page County Census, 1850 and 1860; Slave Schedules, 1850 and 1860. In 1860, John Lionberger (1807–1874) was listed in the Page County census as a "gentleman" living in Luray with over $24,500 in real estate. Out of the three men listed by Isaac Shuler that day at Walton's Newport store, Lionberger was the only slaveholder. John Shuler had owned two slaves in 1850, but by 1860 they had either been emancipated or sold. Though standing against the idea of secession from 1850 to 1860, Lionberger had actually more than doubled the number of slaves he owned, from six to fourteen. Local legend has it that sometime in the latter part of the summer of 1859, while using another name, abolitionist John Brown visited the Lionberger home and began to tell the slaves what they should do once they heard of the impending slave revolt that he was planning. When Lionberger learned of his guest's activities, Brown was immediately thrown out of the house. John Lionberger's only son, John Henry Lionberger (1843–1879), started the war as a lieutenant with the Massanutten Rangers of Company D, Seventh Virginia Cavalry; but by war's end he was a lieutenant in Company C, Thirty-ninth Battalion Virginia Cavalry, a unit noted as General Robert E. Lee's bodyguard and couriers.

James Lee Gillespie (1816–1892) is credited with naming the village of Alma in Page County. As his obituary stated many years after the Civil War, Dr. James L. Gillespie was "a strong southern man [however] he thought secession was wrong and impractical and impolitic and for that reason was arrested." Later transferred to Orange Courthouse, Gillespie was able to escape and later returned to the Valley as a guide for Union General Nathaniel Banks (from March to May 1862) and subsequently for General James Shields (from May to June 1862). By July 1862, Gillespie secured a commission as an assistant surgeon with a West Virginia regiment. After the war, Gillespie was asked to return to Alma as a doctor, but he refused, probably still angered over his treatment as a Unionist. Gillespie died in February 1907 and was buried in Oakwood Cemetery in Tyler County, West Virginia. As sidebar of interest, in 1852 Dr. Gillespie served as one of the five presiding justices over the case of "Jerry," a slave belonging to Colonel Andrew Keyser, who was convicted of an assault on Mr. Keyser's daughter. Jerry was tried on August 23, 1852, and subsequently hanged on September 24, 1852. Do You Remember, *Page News & Courier*, April 9, 1940; Union Army Pension Record for James L. Gillespie, National Archives, Washington, D.C.

Reuben Moore Walton (1818–1894) was originally from Shenandoah County and was a son of Samuel Walton and Sarah McKay. He married Julia Ann Foltz (1821–1891) in 1844. Reuben was a successful merchant in the village of Newport and was listed in the 1860 Page County census with $5,000 in real estate. As most of Julia's brothers were all born prior to 1830, they were all too old for conscription in regular army units. However, three of them—along with Reuben M. Walton—were later conscripted into service with Company B, Eighth Battalion Virginia Reserves. Though Julia's brother Noah served in the reserves, he was also the iron master at Catherine Furnace and was a known Union sympathizer, often assisting Union soldiers in escaping from Page Valley. At one time, however, Confederates dressed as Union soldiers revealed their identities after Foltz had led them out of the area. Foltz was then arrested, but was released on bond to continue to work at the furnace. His good conduct was guaranteed by the bond and the danger of trouble for his relatives if he were to continue his practice of providing an underground railroad to Union soldiers.

10. David Coffman Grayson, "How Co. K Marched Out 50 Years Ago," *Page News & Courier*, June 2, 1911. In writing about his perception of the war as it unfolded, Grayson made a comment that echoed Isaac Shuler's same sentiments in that "From the date of the secession of South Carolina, on to the firing on Fort Sumpter, and the meeting of the Virginia Convention, the majority of the sober, thoughtful citizens of Page were decidedly in favor of the Union and opposed to the suggestion of a disruption by secession, either peaceful or by force, among whom was your scribe. Of course, in the excitement prevailing at that time, there were many impulsive fire eaters, who boasted of their desire to wade thro' blood;—and yet, when the testing time came few of that class were willing or ready even to wade though mid in the weary march!" Isaac Shuler's letters can be found in "Secession Days in Virginia Before the War Broke Out," *Page News & Courier*, August 22, 1939; and "How the War Clouds Broke in Page County," *Page News & Courier*, August 14, 1926.

11. Southern Loyalist Claims, National Archives, Washington, D.C. Individual files of Martin Hite, Morgan M. Price, William H. Sours, Samuel Varner (1814–1898) and Joseph Miller (1825–1905).

12. The Sixty-second Virginia Infantry may have benefited largely by the draft that impacted Page County beginning as early as March 1864. Over half of Second Company M of that regiment was made up of men, young and old, from the county.

13. A son of Lemuel D. (1815–1887) and Mary Ann Getts Alger (1818–1870), Frederick Amos Alger (1842–1886) enlisted with Company M, Eleventh Pennsylvania Cavalry on February 9, 1864, and served throughout the war until discharged at Manchester, Virginia, on August 13, 1865. He returned to Page County after the war, married Sarah Seekford (1842–1911) on March 15, 1866, and the couple had seven children. Of particular interest concerning Alger is that, as one of the designated executors for his will, he chose his friend and neighbor, Jacob D. Koontz.

14. Letter from Isaac Shuler, *Page News & Courier*, August 14, 1926.

15. Ibid. Michael Shuler (1843–1864) left to attend Roanoke College in 1860 as a "partial course" student. With the coming of the war, Shuler opted not to attend the full ten-month session and returned home.

16. Methodist minister and Augusta County-born William David Rippetoe (1835–?) was the first captain of the company but resigned by November 1861. Rippetoe was followed by Ambrose Booton Shenk (1831–1862), who was commissioned as captain on November 28, 1861. Shenk was killed on March 23, 1862, at the battle of Kernstown. Michael Shuler succeeded Shenk in command.

17. The body of Captain Michael Shuler was recovered from the battlefield and was brought home, where it was buried in the Shuler family cemetery. The remains were later removed from the Shuler cemetery and reburied in the St. Paul's Lutheran Church Cemetery. The monument that now stands over the grave was placed by Isaac Shuler in the late 1930s.

18. John D. Aleshire (1821–1862) was a son of Joseph (1796–1849) and Sally Koontz Aleshire (1803–1866). He first married on September 16, 1842, to Elizabeth Ann Shuler (1824–1850), who was a sister to John Shuler. After her death, he married another sister of John Shuler's, Sarah Jane Shuler (1836–1894), on August 28, 1856. In 1860, Aleshire and his wife, along with their two daughters, Sarah E. (1857–1893) and Rebecca J. (1860–1864), were living in Leaksville, District 2. In 1866, after Aleshire's death, Sarah married James E. Morris (1829–?), also a widow and a Confederate Veteran who had served in the Dixie and later

the Purcell Artillery. They moved to Hutchinson, Kansas, in 1884. One of John D. Aleshire's younger brothers, Reuben (1830–1896), served in Company D, Seventh Virginia Cavalry.

19. George Summers Sr. was born February 3, 1812, a son of Michael and Susannah Hershberger Summers.

20. Hiram Philip Strole was born August 17, 1833, a son of Jacob (1789–1860) and Eve Kibler Strole (1800–1882) of Grove Hill. Jacob Strole was a son of Christian Strole (1758–1841), a former Hessian soldier during the American Revolution who had been captured and later indentured to Valentine Kyser, eventually marrying Kyser's daughter, Elizabeth (1769–1854) in 1788. Hiram Strole and Mary Summers were married on November 20, 1856.

21. Hiram Strole would not be the only loss suffered by the Strole family during the war. In 1865, sometime during the last months of the siege of Petersburg, while serving with the Purcell Battery, Hiram's brother, Abraham Strole (born August 28, 1842) was killed in action. Abraham had enlisted early in the war on June 21, 1861, with the locally organized Dixie Artillery and, after it was disbanded in the fall of 1862, he was transferred to the Purcell Battery.

22. Southern Loyalist Claims. The note posted on the door of Summers's store and taken by Union Lieutenant Colonel William Plumb Bacon (1837–1918) is currently in a collection of documents at the Connecticut Historical Society.

23. Ibid. John Welfley (1822–1898) was a wealthy farmer (listed with $16,000 in real estate in the 1860 census) who resided at Shenandoah Iron Works. Born ca. 1847, his oldest son, William F. Welfley, was a member of Captain Thomas Keyser's Company of Virginia Reserves from Page County—a small company made up entirely of seventeen- and eighteen-year-old boys. According to postwar records, William Welfley may have later served late in the war as a member of Company D, Seventh Virginia Cavalry.

24. Following the first Union occupation of Luray in April 1862, a few local pro-secessionists took two civilian men, John F. Haines and a man by the name of Beylor, from their homes for having given aid and comfort to Union officers during their stay in Luray. Lieutenant Colonel Franklin Sawyer of the Eighth Ohio Infantry recalled in a newspaper article that appeared in the *Newark* [Ohio] *Advocate* in 1862 that Haynes had gone "to Washington to attend the inauguration of President Lincoln. He was notified by the rebels not to return, but after the battle of Winchester, and our possession of the Valley, he did return. On our way to Fredericksburg he entertained some of

our officers, and advised with them about his safety. Two days after we left, he was arrested." Both Haines and Beylor were taken to the jail in Luray. Though there is no record of the event in the county court minute books, within days of the arrival of the two men, they were put on trial by a group of local citizens, found guilty of some unspecified crime and condemned to death. "They were taken out of jail at midnight, under pretense of being sent to Richmond, marched about two miles into the woods, and there told that they were to be shot. They were in charge of five of the citizens of Luray, one of whom was a Baptist preacher,—Haynes asked permission to pray, and did so. His prayer was so affecting that the hearts of two of the murderers failed, and one of them seeing this, stepped up and shot Haynes while on his knees, and another one immediately shot Beylor. The bodies were left unburied until our army went up there. The families of these men are said to be in a most wretched condition.—Our Chaplain, Dr. Freeman, visited Mrs. Haynes yesterday, and tells me that she has not left her bed since the murder of her husband was learned by her. This is only one instance out of hundreds, of cruelty of these rebels." The Beylor-Haines execution has become a forgotten event in the history of Page County, but during the Civil War, to local Unionists who remained in the area throughout the war, the tales of the event may have been repeated regularly to Union commands as they occupied the county, causing a great deal of trouble for a large number of citizens, no matter their sympathies.

25. Southern Loyalist Claims. Samuel Step (born ca. 1825) was listed in the 1860 census as living next to George Summers. At the beginning of the war, Step was a corporal in Company L, Ninety-seventh Virginia Militia, but after that unit disbanded, Step appears to have remained out of the military for the balance of the war.

26. Ibid.

27. Ibid. Summers's Loyalist claim was not approved. While he upheld his claims of loyalty through the claims application process, the claims commission's investigator discovered that Summers did aid the Confederacy, whether voluntary or not, on at least two occasions. In December 1861, Summers sold as much as five bushels of wheat and hired out six four-horse wagons and teams for seventeen days at $5 per day and another eight two-horse wagons and three four-horse wagons and teams to the Confederate Army of the Kanawha. In all this amounted to a profit of $1,072. There is no indication whether he actually got these teams back. He also was found to have sold 3,500 pounds of hay and 39½ bushels of wheat to passing Confederates in March 1863.

CHAPTER 2

28. Macon Jordan (1841–1908) served initially as captain of the Massanutten Rangers. After not being reelected in April 1862 and being superceded by schoolmate and Augusta County native Samuel Brown Coyner (1838–1863), Jordan secured a post on the staff of General Robert E. Rodes. He also later served on General Henry Heth's staff and was twice wounded. He died at the Missouri Confederate Home in Higginsville, Missouri, and was buried there.

29. Born December 6, 1844, Jacob Daniel Koontz was the youngest of seven children born to Daniel and Elizabeth Mauck Koontz. There is some confusion over his middle name. Some genealogical references show that his middle name was "Daniel" while Bettie Lee Snyder Koontz (1856–1941), his wife, stated in her widow's pension application that his middle name was "Dallas." Benjamin Drake Guice was the former comrade who referred to Koontz as "Jolly Jake" in one of his letters that appeared in the late 1890s in the *Page News*. Out of his three oldest brothers, Alfred Koontz (1837–1909) is recorded as having served for a brief time in the Confederate service, in Company I, Ninety-seventh Virginia Militia.

30. Andrew Jackson Kite was born ca. 1832 to Daniel and Catherine Kite. On February 20, 1852, he married Rachel R. Secrist (born ca. 1832, a daughter of Jacob Secrist). In 1860, the couple was listed with three children, Madison J. (born ca. 1855), Lydia A.C. (born ca. 1857) and Perry P. (born ca. 1859). Another son, Hiram Tyree Kite, died when only five months old in June 1858. Andrew J. Kite did have two younger brothers, Jacob (born ca. 1838) and Daniel (born ca. 1840). Both may have served for the Confederacy, though records are inconclusive. While there is a reference to Daniel Kite serving in John S. Mosby's Forty-third Battalion Virginia Cavalry, no official record exists. Andrew's other brother, Henry, may have also served, though it is uncertain which units he joined. There is a reference to a Henry Kite as having served in Company H, Ninety-seventh Virginia Militia, and then another reference to a Henry T. Kite as having served in Company E, Ninety-seventh Virginia Militia and later Company F, Twenty-fifth Battalion Virginia Infantry.

There is some confusion as to whether this Andrew Jackson Kite is the one who actually was the one involved in the Summers-Koontz incident. In 1860 there were three men by the name of Andrew Jackson Kite residing in Page County. The aforementioned was one of those men; the other two were born in ca. 1834 and ca. 1836, respectively. However, the one born in 1834 was the only other A.J. Kite residing in Grove Hill in 1860. A son of John and Eve Keyser Kite, he was residing at the home of James and Margaret Conrad Kite. However, the distinction between the two men may actually be found in the Confederate service records. One served in Company D, Seventh Virginia Cavalry while the other served in Company H, Thirty-third Virginia Infantry and died on March 7, 1865, after having been exchanged as a POW from Elmira, New York (from July 1864 to February 1865). A newspaper article in the *Page News & Courier* on January 29, 1924, seems to confuse the matter even further by announcing the death of A. Jackson Kite of Brandy Station, Virginia, and stating that he was "associated with Summers and Koontz in a raid on the federals after the surrender, an exploit that resulted in the capture and judicial murder of the two officers named. Mr. Kite managed to escape from his father's home near Grove Hill when the Yankees came and captured Summers and Koontz." This is, of course, a mistake made by the paper, as this was actually the death of Hiram Jackson Kite (1843–1924), a son of James and Margaret Conrad Kite. Hiram did, however, serve in Company D, Seventh Virginia Cavalry. Hiram J. Kite was paroled in Winchester on May 6, 1865, giving him no reason to be a party to the group that was involved in the episode of May 22, 1865, which led to the executions of Summers and Koontz.

31. By the time that Isaac N. Koontz enlisted, his older brother, Harrison Warren "Judge" Koontz (1834–1910), had only recently been discharged from service in Company I, Ninety-seventh Virginia Militia, having originally enlisted on July 22, 1861. H.W. Koontz later joined Company H, Thirty-third Virginia Infantry on September 23, 1862, and was present through December 1863, at which time he was facing a court martial and was eventually sentenced to loss of pay and thirty-nine lashes. No further record is available after that date. Judge lived in a small dwelling near the A.J. Shuler house and willed most of his property to his brother-in-law after his last remaining sibling, Julia Ann, A.J. Shuler's wife, died in 1873.

32. Isaac Newton Koontz was born on April 3, 1845, the youngest son of Isaac Newton Koontz (1810–1887) and Anna Keyser (1813–1852). He was actually the third in direct lineage in the family to bear the name Isaac Newton Koontz.

33. George Washington Summers was born on December 22, 1843.

34. Three Page Countians matriculated at VMI together in 1848: Hiram

Jackson Strickler (1830–1873), Simeon Beauford Gibbons (1833–1862) and William Overall Yager (1833–1904). While Strickler was dismissed, both Yager and Gibbons graduated in 1852—Yager going on to serve as colonel of the First Texas Cavalry and Gibbons serving as colonel of the Tenth Virginia Infantry. Yager survived the war and returned to Luray in later years, while Gibbons was killed at the battle of McDowell on May 8, 1862.

CHAPTER 3

35. From Mary L. Short's interviews, there was one oral account of the men's intentions stating that "during the war" they "had been given orders by their commanding officer to fall in behind Northern supply trains and escorts and to capture what they could from the Union army and turn the captured property over to the Confederate forces." Then there is yet another account that states that the men had not heard of the surrender of General Lee when they took the horses and other materials. However, neither of these accounts are likely considering that, first, the last commander of the Laurel Brigade, Colonel Elijah V. White, had disbanded the regiments of the brigade within days of Lee's surrender at Appomattox and secondly, word of Lee's surrender was heard in Page County no later than Friday, April 14, 1865, well over a month before the men rode across the Massanutten. First Lieutenant George D. Buswell (1841–1888), Company H, Thirty-third Virginia Infantry, had been at home months in advance of the surrender, still recuperating from a serious wound he had received at Spotsylvania Courthouse in the spring of 1864. On April 14, after traveling through Honeyville and attending a funeral at Mount Zion, while passing through Leaksville, Buswell heard of the surrender and noted it in his diary. A third account states that the men had "found some horses tied to trees and had taken them just for the transportation, intending to return them when they had gotten their own horse from their homes." However, this story is also unlikely and appears to be conjectured over time by one who reflected back upon the old story.

36. If the lieutenant in this party of Federal troopers was actually from Company H, Twenty-second New York Cavalry, it was likely either First Lieutenant William P. Brown or Second Lieutenant Herbert Lord.

Born August 13, 1836, in Van Buren, New York, William P. Brown had previously served in the Second U.S. Cavalry, having enlisted on April 26, 1858, at Harrisburg, Pennsylvania. Initially assigned to Troop F, Second Regiment, U.S. Dragoons, by April 30, 1860, he was reported as present sick at Fort Laramie, Nebraska Territory. This troop changed designation in September or October 1861 and became Company F, Second U.S. Cavalry. On June 27, 1862, during the battle of Gaines Mill, Brown was assigned to special duty and, according to an account given by comrade John Kelly, Brown was busy on this special duty "both day and night without rest until July 2nd when the Army of the Potomac arrived at Harrison's Landing," at which place Brown "was taken down with a severe attack of typhoid fever." When sent to Fortress Monroe to the hospital there, comrade Kelly thought Brown "appeared to be beyond recovery, being wasted to almost a skeleton." Kelly was taken prisoner at Second Manassas/Bull Run and did not see Brown again until February 1863, when Kelly commented that Brown still seemed "much emaciated and hollow eyed from the effects of his sickness." During Stoneman's Raid, Kelly remembered that Brown "was quite prostrated from the fatigue incident to that raid, and when discharged a few days later, by reason of expiration of term of service, W.P. Brown was anything but a strong healthy man." Brown was appointed corporal on November 1, 1862, and in less than a year was mustered out on April 30, 1863, in camp at Deep Creek, Virginia. By January 1864, Brown returned to the army by joining the Twenty-second New York Cavalry, mustering in as first sergeant in Company H on February 2. Brown was promoted a year later, on January 4, 1865, to second lieutenant (with rank from December 21, 1864) and was subsequently promoted again twenty-three days later to first lieutenant, commanding Company D. He mustered out with the company at Winchester, Virginia, on August 1, 1865. Turning to farming as an occupation, on January 4, 1866, Brown married Ina Catherine Roe in Elbridge, New York. The couple had seven children in all (William R., May 13, 1867; David A., October 20, 1868; Grey C., January 31, 1870; Era Ina, November 8, 1875; Edgar P., March 24, 1877; George W., October 5, 1879; John W., March 12, 1883). Ina C. Brown died in Memphis, Onandaga County, New York, on December 3, 1896. William P. Brown died on October 23, 1907.

Born ca. 1841 in New York the son of Ralph Lord (of Connecticut), by 1860, Herbert Lord was living with his father and sister in Watertown Ward 1, Jefferson County, Wisconsin. Serving initially in the First Wisconsin Cavalry, by December 1863 he enlisted with the Twenty-second New York Cavalry. In January 1864, Lord was mustered in as a sergeant. Like Brown, his rise to a lieutenancy took place in 1865 (March), later, for the month of April, being placed in command of Company I. He served with the regiment until it was mustered out at Winchester on August 1, 1865. Herbert Lord did not file a pension and he cannot be located in any census records in years after the war.

37. "Hard Times for Union Men in Page," *Page News & Courier*, June 22, 1933. Among those recorded as having been run out of Page County included the earlier mentioned Gillespie family, Dr. Lawrence Gearing and Thornton H. Taylor and his son Daniel (who joined a Union infantry regiment from Kentucky). Jacob H. Coffman once noted that, though not run out, John M. Keyser (1810–1872) was taken to the top of the Blue Ridge at Milam's Gap, stood on a barrel "with a rope around his neck and eased him down, but did not intend to kill him. The purpose of this harsh treatment was to scare him. The torture was enough to render him unable to read for three months. How he made his way home, I never heard, but I surely believe he never identified his captors."

38. The letter referring to Butterfield was written to the governor and the adjutant general of Ohio from Camp Keys, Romney, Virginia, on October 30, 1861, and was from John S. Mason, colonel, Commanding Post, and Edwin B. Olmstead, captain, Company H, Fourth Ohio Infantry. It was stated in the same letter that they both believed Butterfield was "qualified for any position which might be vacant in his regiment."

39. Francis Wellington Butterfield was born ca. 1830 in Coloese, Oswego County, New York, to Amory and Mary Lamb Butterfield. The Butterfield family was of old Pilgrim stock, emigrating from England to Massachusetts sometime in the 1630s. From there, the family moved to Vermont, New York State and eventually, with Francis W. Butterfield, to Ohio. In the same family line, Francis was also a third cousin to Union General Daniel Adams Butterfield, famous for having composed "Taps," in 1862. Francis W. Butterfield had been previously married and had one son, Frank (born 1851), when he married Rachel Reid Foster (of Crawford, Ohio) on May 12, 1856, at Bucyrus, Ohio. Census records for Eden Township, Seneca County, Ohio, identify a twenty-one-year-old Francis W. Butterfield residing with his wife Hersula. However, this same record shows that Butterfield was born in Massachusetts, not in New York. His wife is identified in the census records as having been born in New York. Yet another census record for Butterfield for 1860 stated that he was born in Vermont.

40. This was also the only time that Butterfield was recorded as having received a wound. According to his declaration for invalid pension, dated November 23, 1864, Butterfield was "accidentally wounded in the following way; that while detached from the balance of his regiment, and stationed at Cumberland, Md. being ordered by Capt. Hagans, commanding the post, on or about the 15th of Aug. 1861 to arrest certain rebel citizens of that city and while discharging that duty, he received

word that one of said citizens was leaving the city in great haste, and in the direction of the enemies lines, and ordering his 2nd Lieut (Hysung) with a squad of men to proceed to arrest him forthwith, and that the said Lieut Hysung after proceeding some distance in the discharge of this duty returned to him (the captain) to borrow his revolver, as the man to be arrested was reported to the Lieut as being a desperado, and that while he (the captain) was drawing his revolver to give the Lieut it accidentally discharged, and its contents passed through the center of his right hand entirely disabling him from working at his trade which is the carpenter business."

CHAPTER 4

41. The only William Tharp listed in Page County census records was William Henry Tharp (1813–1885) of District 4, Luray. However, it is unlikely that this was the William Tharp involved in this affair. There was, however, a James Tharp—a seventy-three year-old distiller—residing at Newport in 1860. Though not listed with the family, it seems possible that the William Tharp involved in this incident may have been related to if not actually a son of this James Tharp (born in Fauquier County, Virginia, ca. 1787) and his wife Nancy Skelton Tharp (born ca. 1814, the daughter of William Skelton and Mary Batchelder of Shenandoah County, Virginia). James and Nancy were married on August 9, 1830, in Shenandoah County. The four children of this couple that were listed in the 1860 Page County census were all born between the years of 1834 and 1851. While residents of Newport in 1860, this particular Tharp family appears neither in the 1850 or 1870 census records for Page County.
42. "A Noble Family of Page," Do You Remember, *Page News & Courier*, June 1938.
43. A slight variation, and possibly embellished, version of the Isaac Shuler account here was mentioned by Mary L. Short in her paper where her source stated that "Jacob Koontz was there escorting a girl in whom the Tharp boy was also interested. During the afternoon fellowship period Tharp, in the course of conversation, said to Jacob Koontz that he ought to go over and steal some more Northern horses. Jake got angry and hit Tharp who proceeded to go over the mountain and report to the Federal camp that these same young men who had taken the horses were 'breaking the peace and dignity of the truce.'" Though an interesting variation, in that Isaac Shuler was an eyewitness, his account is likely more accurate.

44. Tharp's actions and outward exertions of contempt toward the Kite brothers in this argument and his subsequent trip to the Union camp at Rude's Hill is not very different from that of Thornton Hamilton Taylor in a statement that he made upon his return to Page County in June 1865. The end of the war and the surrender of the Army of Northern Virginia seem to have considerably empowered local Unionists in their general actions towards those who had supported the Confederacy in one way or another. Of course, after the manner in which they had been treated by radical "fire-eating secessionists" in the first two years of the war, this is not surprising. Jacob H. Coffman, "More of the Summers and Koontz Affair," *Page News & Courier*, June 1933. Coffman recalled Taylor's return to Page and said that "During the half hour Mr. Taylor stopped to chat with my parents he took occasion to say, 'I'd like to see them chase me away from my home now.' He later became postmaster at Marksville—another case of the bottom rail getting on top."

45. "Sketch of Allen W. Kite and a Noble Family," *Page News & Courier*, December 1, 1923. St. Paul's Lutheran Church was in its last phases of construction by the end of the war, its congregation having relocated from its former church site known as Monger's Church, just to the southeast of the new church and along the South Fork of the Shenandoah River. There are some who have stated that this could not have taken place at St. Paul's because the church was still not completed by 1865; however, again, Isaac Shuler's firsthand accounting seems to indicate otherwise. The congregation officially met on July 7, 1860, and appointed a building committee, one of the members being John Shuler. Two weeks later, the committee had decided on building a structure that would be thirty-eight-by-fifty feet. The building was not officially dedicated until November 31, 1868. Reverend W.H. Cone was pastor of the congregation during the war.

Benjamin M. Kite (1839–1912) and Lewis Wolford Kite (1846–1922) both served as Confederate soldiers. Benjamin enlisted in 1861 with Company H, Thirty-third Virginia Infantry and served regularly until captured at Spotsylvania Courthouse on May 12, 1864. Sent to Fort Delaware as a prisoner of war, he was exchanged on February 27, 1865. Lewis was originally a member of Captain Thomas Keyser's Boy Company of Virginia Reserves. Like several in Keyser's Company, Lewis later enlisted or was conscripted in Second Company M, Sixty-second Virginia Mounted Infantry, and likely saw service at the battle of New Market on May 15, 1864. Listed as absent without leave in October 1864 and with records being incomplete for the Sixty-second after that time, it is unknown whether or not he served until the close of the war. Both Benjamin and Lewis were sons of Noah and Isabella Pirkey Kite. Both parents and three of their youngest siblings were victims of the tragic flood that devastated the area around Alma in 1870. Noah Kite's Mill was known as Columbia Mill, from whence the bridge near Alma gained its name. One of Noah and Isabella Kite's daughters married the aforementioned Isaac Shuler.

46. Morning Order Books of the 192nd Ohio Volunteer Infantry, National Archives, Washington, D.C. Per Butterfield's service records with the 192nd Ohio, he went on furlough back to Ohio pursuant to paragraph 1, Special Order 45, Army of the Shenandoah. Not long after Butterfield's departure, on June 21 a John L. Arnold was accused of horse thievery and the execution of General Order 1 was considered. However, a witness against Arnold was not very credible and the proposed execution was suspended.

47. Lycurgus D. Lusk was born ca. 1837 and enlisted in Company I, Seventeenth New York Infantry on May 10, 1861, as a sergeant. He was discharged on June 2, 1863. He later joined Company H, Twenty-second New York Cavalry on February 6, 1864, and was appointed first lieutenant on March 30, 1864. Lusk was later appointed as captain on July 27, 1864, and was actively involved in the Shenandoah Valley Campaign of 1864 and participated in the battle of Waynesboro in March 1865. He was mustered out with the company on August 1, 1865, at Winchester, Virginia. He appears to have been brevetted as a major of U.S. Volunteers from March 13, 1865.

48. Morning Order Book.

49. S.E. Williams and D.D. Worth, eds., Cyrus Hussey Diary Website. www.48ovvi.org/oh48hussey.html.

50. Beginning with Captain Christopher Hussey, the Hussey family left England for America in the 1630s. A settler in the Massachusetts Bay Colony, by the 1650s, Hussey became influenced by Society of Friends missionaries, though it is believed that he never joined. His sons however, did join the Quaker faith. Six years after the death of Christopher Hussey in Hampton, New Hampshire, son John migrated to New Castle, Delaware, in 1692. Remaining in Delaware for several generations, by the 1760s another Christopher Hussey, the great-grandson of Captain Christopher Hussey, migrated to Guilford County, North Carolina. The family remained in North Carolina for three more generations before Lieutenant Colonel Cyrus Hussey's father moved to Ohio around 1808.

51. Cyrus Hussey website. As a bit of irony, Captain George W. Summers was descended from Quakers on his mother's side of the family; Valentine Hollingsworth (1632–1710) is believed to have become a Quaker around 1660. He immigrated to America in 1682 and, prior to the arrival of the Hussey family in the same place, settled in New Castle, Delaware. His grandson, Abraham Hollingsworth, built "Abraham's Delight," now more commonly known as "Abram's Delight," which is located in Winchester, Virginia. Abraham's grandson, also named Abraham (born ca. 1748), was disowned by the Quaker faith for having driven a supply wagon in the American Revolution. This Abraham Hollingsworth was Captain George W. Summers's great-grandfather.

52. Ibid. Florence Anna Hussey was born April 19, 1861, and died on August 12, 1861.

53. Ibid.

54. Ibid.

55. Ibid.

Chapter 5

56. An oral account given to Ms. Short states that this was a "bright moonlit night." However, a new moon had just occurred on June 23 and therefore there was no natural light available.

57. Home of the Birds, *Page News & Courier*, June 1933. In Seekford's recalling the words of I.N. Koontz, the mention of "Aunt Betty" refers to Elizabeth "Betty" Mauck Koontz (1805–1877), Daniel Koontz's wife and Jacob Daniel Koontz's mother. Seekford also noted they remembered Isaac Newton Koontz's words from that time. "I have been at the Koontz home when the old clock would strike and old Mrs. Koontz would cry like a child. Newton Koontz's sweetheart, whom he was engaged to, would visit the home to hear the old clock strike where she would sit and weep." Speaking more of the clock, Seekford noted that, at the time of the writing, "This clock is about a hundred and fifty years old and is now owned by Millard [A.] Strole [1871–1946] who has it in his silver shop in rooms above the Cash Store at Stanley. Mr. Strole bought this old clock when it had been junked and no longer kept time. It is now in perfect running order and if you would go to Stanley and sit down there at the post office, you could hear it strike and tell the hour of the day." Seekford also commented that when the clock was still at the old Daniel Koontz home, in that the home was "about fifty yards from the public road" and "when it was near time

for the clock to strike," people would "stop out in front of the house and listen to the striking of the old clock. I have seen men sit on their horses and weep when this old clock would hammer off the hours."

58. Mary L. Short, "Information Collected Relating to the Execution of Sergeant Isaac Newton Koontz and Captain George W. Summers," (research paper, James Madison University, December 1, 1977).

59. Socrates Henkel (1823–1901) was married to Eleanora Caroline Henkel. Eleanora was, through her mother (Mary, daughter of Martin Kite), a first cousin to Jacob Daniel Koontz.

60. Assuming that Lusk's detachment was made up of men from his company, it is interesting to note that the lieutenant who gave into Summers's and Koontz's appeals on June 27 may have been the same lieutenant who refused to give up his horse on May 22; or it was the other lieutenant who had not been present on May 22. In either case, it appears that it could have either been First Lieutenant William D. Brown or Second Lieutenant Herbert Lord.

61. At the time of the execution, this property was owned by Henry Neff Kagey (1804–1879), a son of Abraham (1764–1831) and Anna Neff Kagey (1772–1828). Located on the southernmost edge of what is more commonly known as "Rude's Hill," the nearby Kagey home place known as "Locust Vale" probably dates to the late 1700s–early 1800s, well before the Lutheran minister Andrew R. Rude had any association with the hill. It is believed that all of Abraham Anna Kagey's children were born here beginning as early as 1802. One of Henry N. Kagey's sons, John Henry Kagey (1842–1895), served in the Eighth Star New Market Artillery during the war and is buried in Cedar Grove Cemetery, which is just to the north of the Summers-Koontz Monument. Henry Neff Kagey, through his brother, Abraham Neff Kagey (1807–1893), also had a famous nephew named John Henri Kagi (1835–1859). A close associate of abolitionist John Brown, Kagi was born in Brisolville, Ohio, and from 1854 to 1855 he taught school at Hawkinstown, Virginia, which is just north of Mount Jackson in Shenandoah County. While in Hawkinstown, it is said that Kagi gained a personal knowledge of slavery, and because of his outspoken antislavery views, was forced to leave in haste. He later joined John Brown in Kansas and bore the title of secretary of war in Brown's provisional government. Kagi was killed in the attack on Harpers Ferry on October 17, 1859.

Rude's Hill was originally owned by William Steenbergen Jr. and, he, his wife (the former Elizabeth Caperton of Monroe County, Virginia/West Virginia) and child lived in the house that is situated on the northern edge of Rude's Hill and just on the edge of Meem's Bottom. Steenbergen died in 1834 and, in 1844, his widow married Lutheran minister Andrew Rudolph Rude, a native of Copenhagen, Denmark. The Rude family made their home at the old Steenbergen home and, apparently the name "Rude's Hill" became affiliated with the area sometime after 1844.

62. Jacob H. Coffman (1852–1938) was the youngest son of Jacob (1803–?) and Judith Hurt Coffman (ca. 1808–ca. 1852) and was a frequent contributor of local history to the *Page News & Courier* in the early part of the twentieth century. All four of his older brothers served in locally raised Confederate companies.

Upon her return trip to Page County, Jane Hurt Weakley (1846–?) was the widow of John Weakley (1833–?), who had "gone west before the war and was killed in the army." The couple had been married at Mill Creek on January 19, 1863, he being the son of William and Lucy Cave Weakley and she the daughter of Simeon and Biddy Smith Hurt. She later (October 9, 1866) married Henry Abner Cave (1846–?). There is a John Weakley listed with Company L, Tenth Virginia Infantry but there is no further record of him after he was listed as absent without leave as of September 12, 1863. Home of the Birds, *Page News & Courier*, July 1933.

63. "More on the Summers and Koontz Affair," *Page News & Courier*, July 4, 1933. Jacob Coffman's account was slightly mistaken in that he said that the execution took place on Sunday morning.

64. Whitelaw Reid, *Ohio in the War: Her Statesmen, Generals and Soldiers*, vol. 2. (Columbus, OH: Eclectic Publishing, 1893), 737. There was an oral account related to Mary L. Short that states that Newton Koontz had asked not to be shot in the face "because his sweetheart would have to 'look on him' and he didn't want her to see him that way, but both were shot in the face after all." There is no information available in support of this oral story and it would seem that George Summers Sr. would very well have made some sort of comment about this in his lengthy article if something like this would have taken place.

65. One of Ms. Short's informants told her that James L. Gillespie, mentioned earlier in this book, had been called to help the boys in their dilemma, in that he had "the respect of the Union government was on his way to New Market but did not arrive in time." At the time, Gillespie was on duty in Philadelphia, so this seems most unlikely.

66. Andrew Jackson Shuler (1831–1911) was a younger brother of the aforementioned John Shuler and was married in 1850 to Julia Ann Koontz (1836–1873), daughter of Isaac Newton Koontz II (1810–1887)

and sister of Sergeant I.N. Koontz. By 1860, the A.J. Shuler family was living at the Isaac Newton Koontz homestead. Lieutenant George D. Buswell noted that he attended the burials of both Summers and Koontz on Thursday, June 29. Busy in his farming endeavors, Buswell first learned of the incident when he had gone over to Gideon C. Brubaker's on June 28 to obtain a rake. Buswell noted in his diary on that same day that he had heard about "the sad news of the execution of the gallant and noble young Capt. Geo. W. Summers & Sergt. I.N. Koontz."

CHAPTER 6

67. "Rev. Socrates Henkel's Experience in Page," *Page News & Courier*, July 26, 1927. The story was brought to the attention of the paper when Mr. Elon O. Henkel, a son of Reverend Henkel, was traveling through Luray on Saturday, July 23, 1927. Reverend Henkel's diary was then in the possession of Elon.

68. Henry Beeby was twenty-four years old when he enlisted on June 13, 1861, at Syracuse. Initially serving with Company B, Third New York Cavalry, he was later promoted to sergeant and reenlisted as a veteran in January 1864, mustering in as second lieutenant of Company F, Twenty-second New York Cavalry. He was captured in some unnamed action but was paroled and returned to duty. Beeby was promoted to first lieutenant in April 1865 and remained with the Twenty-second New York Cavalry until mustered out at Winchester on August 1, 1865. Beeby married shortly after the war. In 1880, he, along with his wife, Catherine, was listed as residing in Hastings, Oswego County, New York, with children Florence (1866), Mary (1868), Charles (1870), Nellie (1873), Kittie (1875) and Fred (1879). He died sometime between 1920 and 1921. Regretfully, Beeby's pension application is missing from the files of the National Archives. His wife, Catherine, applied for a widow's pension in 1921.

69. Jeffry D. Wert, *Mosby's Rangers*. (New York: Simon & Schuster, 1990). On September 23, 1864, Torbert ordered the execution of six of Colonel John S. Mosby's Rangers in retaliation for an attack on a train of ambulance wagons, but more specifically for the death of a lieutenant in the same attack near Front Royal. In Mosby's absence, the order for the attack had been given by Captain William Henry Chapman, Mosby's second-in-command, to his older brother, Captain Samuel Forrer Chapman. Both Chapmans actually hailed from Luray. The attack went afoul when the Confederates realized they were attacking

the van of what was actually a retrograde march of Torbert's entire two divisions. Six of Mosby's troopers were captured; four were shot and two were hanged.

70. Three of the remaining Summers daughters married men of Company D, Seventh Virginia Cavalry. Barbara Ann Summers (1835–1899) married Gordianus Dovel (1830–1907) on November 4, 1851. Gordianus Dovel was a member of Company L, Ninety-seventh Virginia Militia. Sarah Jane Summers (1840–1916) married David F. Dovel (1836–1907) on September 19, 1865. David Dovel had been a third sergeant with the Rangers and was severely wounded at Ream's Station in August 1864. Susan C. Summers (1845–1912) married Peter C. Reid (1837–1915) on January 21, 1864. Reid had served as constable in Alma, residing with the family of Reuben M. Walton in 1860, and at the opening of the war was serving as a major in the Ninety-seventh Virginia Militia. After joining Company D, he was elected second lieutenant. He was "shown the white feather" for cowardice at the battle of McDowell on May 8, 1862, and subsequently submitted his resignation in July, but it was rejected. He was captured less than a month later, was exchanged and returned to duty as a first lieutenant by November 1862. However, he was frequently sick and absent from duty due to hemorrhaging of the lungs and again submitted his resignation. A medical examination found him to be suffering from phthisis pulmonalis. His resignation was accepted in December 1863.

71. A.J. and Julia Koontz Shuler's daughter and eighth child, Emma Jane Shuler (1868–1937) married John Robert Sutphin (1846–1914) in 1899. A widow, Sutphin was born in Fauquier County to Barnet and Mary Sutphin. He was also a Confederate Veteran, having served in Company B, Sixth Virginia Cavalry.

72. Children of John Layton and Emma Jane Shuler Strole included Etta Florence Strole (1869–1924), Clara Virginia Strole (1872–1954), Aramitta Strole (1875–1960), Anna Belle Strole (1877–1878), Jacob Lorom Strole (1879–1967), William Arthur Strole (1881–?) and James Clarence Strole (1886–?).

73. Emma Jane Shuler Strole was buried beside her husband and near her parents in St. Paul's Lutheran Church Cemetery in Grove Hill.

74. Andrew Jackson Kite was buried in a small cemetery at Ingham, near Grove Hill. Andrew's widow, Rebecca, filed for a Confederate widow's pension on March 4, 1909.

75. Bettie Snyder was the daughter of John W. Snyder (1827–1870) and Cinderella Dovel (1832–1861). John W. Snyder served initially in the war as a private in Company M, Ninety-seventh Virginia Militia.

76. Jacob D. Koontz was buried in Evergreen Cemetery, Luray, Virginia. On May 1, 1926, twenty-two years after Jacob's death, Bettie Koontz filed for a Confederate widow's pension. She was awarded $22.50 per month.

77. Children of Jacob D. and Bettie L. Koontz included Frank Lester Koontz (1877–1945), Hollie Bessie Koontz (1879–?), Lelia Garnet Koontz Hite (1881–1967) and Fred Snyder Koontz (1888–1926).

78. Butterfield was residing at 1009 Baltimore Avenue in Kansas City, Missouri, when he applied for an increase to his invalid pension on February 20, 1883. His widow was residing at 814 Harrison Street, Kansas City, Missouri, on June 25, 1894, when she applied for a pension. At that time she claimed that she owned no real estate or personal property, bonds, stocks or other investments" and that there were "no person or persons legally bound for her support, and she derives no income from any source or sources whatsoever." Following the death of Rachel Butterfield, the family's financial status was still in dire straits. One daughter, Chancey G. Butterfield (born ca. 1869) (Lucy or Lula was born ca. 1858 and Pardie or Parda was born ca. 1859), wrote the commissioner of pensions on January 30, 1896, just over three weeks after her mother's death on January 4, and asked if the three children were entitled to the unpaid accrued pension of sixteen dollars. Miss Butterfield wrote, "She left three children, two sons and a daughter. My oldest brother is in California, where he has been for about five years, during which time he has not contributed toward the support of his mother, and since my father's death, the entire support of my mother and sister has fallen upon my shoulders, and we have always depended upon 'Uncle Sam's' financial appreciation of my patriotic father's services to assist us in paying our house rent, etc. and now that it is entirely cut off, I should like to receive at least the accrued pension, which would materially assist me in defraying my mother's funeral expense, at least."

79. Lusk applied for a veteran's pension on March 26, 1890.

80. Rebecca Hodson Hussey died on February 17, 1870; Florence E. Hussey was born June 28, 1846, in Sidney, Ohio; James Whittlesey Hussey was born May 16, 1878; Arthur Duncan Hussey was born March 5, 1882.

81. At the time Hussey applied for a pension he was residing at 2323 Robinswood Avenue, having moved not long before from 1531 Cherry Street. After his death, his widow, Frances E. Hussey, applied for a pension on October 15, 1926. Cyrus Hussey was buried in Forest Cemetery in Toledo. His wartime diary, covering the period from July 1862 to December 1864, is on file with the Ward M. Cannaday Center for Special Collections at the University of Toledo.

CHAPTER 7

82. John W. Wayland, *A History of Shenandoah County, Virginia* (Strasburg, VA: Shenandoah Publishing House, 1927). According to Wayland, "for many years a stout locust post marked the place of execution in the Kagey field."

83. "The Soldiers Cenotaph," *Shenandoah Valley*, June 29, 1893.

84. Israel was also mayor of Shenandoah and ran a professional photography studio in the town. Maryland-born, Israel had served in Virginia artillery units during the war, including Company B, First Virginia Light Artillery, J.S. Brown's Battery (Wise Artillery) and O.B. Taylor's Battery. Miller is believed to have served in Company D, Thirty-fourth Virginia Infantry.

85. Wyant served as a corporal in Company E, Tenth Virginia Infantry.

86. From the available list of members of the original Summers-Koontz Camp, it appears that Koontz may well have been the only member in 1904 who was actually a descendant and real son of a soldier from Company D, Seventh Virginia Cavalry. Amiss's father, Major Thomas Benjamin Amiss, had started the war as a member of the Sixth Virginia Cavalry but served most of the war as a surgeon in various units and hospitals; Adams's father, Robert Stribling Adams, is believed to have been a member of Company K, Seventh Virginia Infantry; McKim's father, Albert W. McKim, was a member of Company C, Forty-third Battalion Virginia Cavalry, Colonel John S. Mosby's Rangers; Wright was the son of Silas K. Wright, Company E, Twelfth Virginia Cavalry; Reverend Kennard was the son of Major Michael Shelby Kennard, Company C, First Arkansas Volunteers and the Fifteenth Texas Cavalry; Price was the son of Charles David Price, Company C, Thirty-fifth Battalion Virginia Cavalry; Cary is believed to have been the son of Edward F. Cary, Company G, Forty-ninth Virginia Infantry; Booton was the son of Captain John Kaylor Booton of the Dixie Artillery from Page County; little is known about Dr. Willis or who his father may have been.

87. At the time of Mr. Rosen's death in 2004, he was a member of the Captain Jack Adams Camp 1951, Sons of Confederate Veterans based in Edinburg, in Shenandoah County, Virginia.

88. In contrast with the organization from 1904 was the fact that out of the seven charter members of the re-chartered camp of 1999, there were four members who were direct descendants from members of Company D, Seventh Virginia Cavalry. As of 2005–06 membership year, more

than half of the camp's nearly thirty members are lineally or collaterally descended from members of Captain Summers's Massanutten Rangers.

Bibliography

NEWSPAPERS

Newark Advocate, Newark, Ohio
Page Courier, Luray, Virginia
Page News, Luray, Virginia
Page News & Courier, Luray, Virginia
Rockingham Register, Harrisonburg, Virginia
The Shenandoah Valley, New Market, Virginia
Staunton Spectator, Staunton, Virginia

Manuscript Sources

Compiled Service Records of Confederate Soldiers who Served in Organizations from the state of Virginia, National Archives, Washington, D.C.

Morning Order Book of the 192nd Ohio Volunteer Infantry, National Archives, Washington, D.C.

Papers of Lieutenant Colonel William Plumb Bacon (1837–1918), Connecticut Historical Society, Hartford.

Pension Records of Union Veterans, National Archives, Washington, D.C.

Population Schedules for the Seventh Census of the United States, 1850, for Page County, Virginia, National Archives, Washington, D.C.

Population Schedules for the Eighth Census of the United States, 1860, for Page County, Virginia, National Archives, Washington, D.C.

Records of the Circuit Court of Page County, Virginia, Library of Virginia, Richmond.

Slave Schedules for Page County, Virginia, 1850 and 1860, National Archives, Washington, D.C.

Southern Loyalist Claims, National Archives, Washington, D.C.

Virginia Confederate Disability Applications, Library of Virginia, Richmond.

Virginia Confederate Pension Applications, Library of Virginia, Richmond.

Work Projects Administration Historical Inventory of Page County, Virginia, Library of Virginia, Richmond.

Published Sources

Armstrong, Richard L. *7th Virginia Cavalry*. Lynchburg, VA: H.E. Howard, 1992.

Burns, Michael G. *From Rochester to Winchester: The Regimental History of the 22nd New York Cavalry, 1864–1865*. Westminster, MD: Heritage Books, 2001.

Chamberlin, W.H., ed. *War of War History, 1861–1865, Papers Prepared for the Ohio Commandery of the Military Order of the Loyal Legion of the United States, 1890–1896*. Cincinnati, OH: Robert Clarke Company, 1896.

Delaughter, Roger U., Jr. *62nd Virginia Infantry*. Lynchburg, VA: H.E. Howard, 1988.

Divine, John E. *35th Battalion Virginia Cavalry*. Lynchburg, VA: H.E. Howard, 1985.

Driver, Robert J., Jr., and Ruffner, Kevin C. *1st Battalion Virginia Infantry, 39th Battalion Virginia Cavalry, 24th Battalion Virginia Partisan Rangers*. Lynchburg, VA: H.E. Howard, 1996.

Dulfour, Charles L. *Gentle Giant: The Gallant Life of Roberdeau Wheat*. Baton Rouge: Louisiana State University Press, 1957.

Eisenberg, William Edward. *The Lutheran Church in Virginia, 1717–1962, Including an Account of the Lutheran Church in East Tennessee*. Roanoke, VA: Trustees of the Virginia Synod Lutheran Church in America, 1967.

Hewett, Janet B. et al., eds. *Supplement to the Official Records of the Union and Confederate Armies*. 100 volumes. Wilmington, NC: Broadfoot Publishing, 1994.

Jordan, Cornelia Jane Matthews. *Echoes from the Cannon*. Buffalo, NY: Charles Wells Moulton, 1899.

Keen, Hugh C., and Mewborn, Horace. *43rd Battalion Virginia Cavalry: Mosby's Command*. Lynchburg, VA: H.E. Howard, 1993.

Kerkhoff, Jennie Ann. *Old Homes of Page County, Virginia*. Luray, VA: Lauck and Company, 1962.

Kleese, Richard B. *Shenandoah County in the Civil War: The Turbulent Years*. Lynchburg, VA: H.E. Howard, 1992.

Koontz, Lowell L. *History of the Descendants of John Koontz*. Parsons, WV: McClain Printing Company, 1979.

Layman, Kathryn Foltz. *The Christian Strole History: 1776–1983*. N.p., n.d.

Miles, Dudley H., ed. *The Photographic History of the Civil War*, Vol. 1–10. New York: The Review of Reviews, 1911.

Moore, Robert H., II. *Avenue of Armies: Civil War Sites and Stories of Luray and Page County, Virginia*. Virginia Beach, VA: Donning Co. Publishers, 2002.

———. *The Danville, Eighth Star New Market and Dixie Artillery*. Lynchburg, VA: H.E. Howard, 1989.

————. *Short Historical Sketches of Page County, Virginia and Its People.* Westminster, MD: Heritage Books, 2005.

Murphy, Terrance V. *10th Virginia Infantry.* Lynchburg, VA: H.E. Howard, 1989.

Musick, Michael P. *6th Virginia Cavalry.* Lynchburg, VA: H.E. Howard, 1990.

Myers, Frank M. *The Comanches: A History of White's Battalion, Virginia Cavalry.* Baltimore, MD: Kelly, Piet & Co., 1871.

Page County Bicentennial Commission. *Page: The County of Plenty.* Luray, VA: privately published, 1976.

Portraits of Companions of the Commandery of the State of Ohio, Military Order of the Loyal Legion of the United States. Wilmington, NC: Broadfoot Company, 1993.

Reid, Whitelaw. *Ohio in the War: Her Statesmen, Generals and Soldiers*, vol. 2. Columbus, OH: Eclectic Publishing, 1893.

Reidenbaugh, Lowell. *33rd Virginia Infantry.* Lynchburg, VA: H.E. Howard, 1987.

Short, Mary L. "Information Collected Relating to the Execution of Sergeant Isaac Newton Koontz and Captain George W. Summers" (research paper, James Madison University, December 1, 1977).

Strickler, Harry M. *A Short History of Page County, Virginia.* Harrisonburg, VA: C.J. Carrier Company, 1985.

U.S. War Department. *The War of the Rebellion: A Compilation of the Official Records of the Union and Confederate Armies.* 128 volumes. Washington, D.C.: U.S. War Department, 1880–1901.

Virginia County Vote on the Secession Ordinance, May 23, 1861. Richmond: Library of Virginia, unpublished.

Wallace, Lee A., Jr. *A Guide to Virginia Military Organizations, 1861–1865.* Lynchburg, VA: H.E. Howard, 1988.

Warner, Ezra J. *Generals in Blue: Lives of the Union Commanders*. Baton Rouge: Louisiana State University Press, 1964.

Wayland, John W. *A History of Rockingham County, Virginia*. Harrisonburg, VA: C.J. Carrier, 1912.

————. *A History of Shenandoah County, Virginia*. Strasburg, VA: Shenandoah Publishing House, 1927.

————. *Stonewall Jackson's Way*. Staunton, VA: McClure Printing, 1969.

Wert, Jeffrey D. *From Winchester to Cedar Creek: The Shenandoah Campaign of 1864*. Carlisle, PA: South Mountain Press, 1987.

Williams, S.E., and D.D. Worth, eds. Cyrus Hussey Diary Website. http://www.48ovvi.org/oh48husseydiary.html.

————. *Mosby's Rangers*. New York: Simon and Schuster, 1990.

Index

Portion of a map of Page County (1862) by Jedediah Hotchkiss. Note that Grove Hill was mistakenly identified as Bunker Hill. The John Shuler house is shown on the map just to the northwest of Bunker Hill. George Summers's store and Somerville Heights are just to the east of Bunker Hill. Alma is obscured by an ink blot on the original map and is near Columbia Bridge. Rude's Hill is near the upper lefthand corner. Courtesy of the Library of Congress.

About the Author

Robert H. Moore II received his Bachelor of Science degree in liberal studies from Excelsior College and is currently completing his thesis for his MA in history from Old Dominion University. Mr. Moore has written seven books (from 1989 to 1999) covering the histories of twenty-seven Virginia artillery batteries for the Virginia Regimental History Series as well as *Avenue of Armies: Civil War Sites and Stories of Luray and Page County, Virginia* (2002) and *Gibraltar of the Shenandoah Valley: Civil War Sites and Stories of Staunton, Waynesboro and Augusta County, Virginia* (2004). He has also maintained the "Heritage & Heraldry" column for the *Page News & Courier* (Luray, Virginia) for the past nine years and from these articles has, to date, produced three additional volumes: *Short Historical Sketches of Page County, Virginia and Its People*. He also contributed several articles to various magazines including *Civil War Times Illustrated*, *Blue and Gray Magazine* and *America's Civil War*. In addition, Mr. Moore has served on the History Committee for Virginia Civil War Trails (1999–2003) and the Education & Interpretation Committee of the Shenandoah Valley Battlefields Foundation (2000–2003). He also served as grants writer (1999–2001) and development director (2001–2002) for the Frontier Culture Museum of Virginia. Mr. Moore currently serves as commander of several Civil War-related heritage groups in Page County, including the Summers-Koontz Camp No. 490, Sons of Confederate Veterans; the Immortal 600 Chapter No. 298, Military Order of the Stars and Bars; and the Luray-Carlisle Reunion Camp No. 1881, Sons of Union Veterans of the Civil War. As he points out in "A Note to the Reader," Moore is also related to several of the key persons in the story of the Summers-Koontz incident. In addition to being a third great-grandson to Emma Jane Shuler, he is also a distant cousin to both Sergeant Isaac Newton Koontz and Captain George W. Summers. Currently a stay-at-home father, Mr. Moore resides with his wife and children in Augusta County, Virginia, in the historic Shenandoah Valley.